BIRMINGHAM BEER

A HEADY HISTORY OF BREWING IN THE MAGIC CITY

CARLA JEAN WHITLEY

AMERICAN PALATE

Published by American Palate
A Division of The History Press
Charleston, SC 29403
www.historypress.net

Cover image by Rachel Callahan, picturebirmingham.com.

First published 2015

Manufactured in the United States

ISBN 978.1.62619.456.4

Library of Congress Control Number: 2015937276

To Free the Hops members, past and present, for lobbying the state legislature to allow so many new and exciting beers into our market

CONTENTS

ACKNOWLEDGEMENTS

This is what it's really like to write a book:

Receiving an e-mail from a pub owner (Jerry Hartley) after an editor says to him, "We think one of your patrons is probably the right author for this book."

Months holed up in archives and digital collections (Birmingham Public Library, Alabama Media Group), poring over the reporting and research of those who came before you.

Relying on your roommate (Sara Samchok) to take the trash and recycling to the curb for weeks on end because you don't have the mental bandwidth to remember.

Conversations about dreams fulfilled over a beer at your neighborhood brewery (Good People, Avondale, Cahaba and Trim Tab brewing companies) or pub (the J. Clyde).

Asking those who were involved (Danner Kline) what it felt like to listen to hours upon hours of debate in legislative session.

Chasing the sun on a photo shoot and insisting your photographer (Rachel Callahan) take her first sips of beer.

Sharing research over a beer lunch (Bill Plott).

Desperately seeking advice from your personal librarians (Marliese Thomas, Amber Long and Kelsey Scouten Bates).

Looking in the bathroom mirror halfway through the workday and realizing you forgot to put on mascara, again.

Acknowledgements

Taking in stories from those who paved the path before your generation's (Steve Betts).

Skipping out on way too many yoga classes (Melissa Scott, Sacred Glow YTT class of '14) in favor of slumping over a laptop on the couch.

Searching for five minutes in which you can take a break and clip your toenails without guilt.

Recalling the first visit to your favorite beer bar with a friend (Murray Sexton Gervais) who was quick to claim it as your shared spot even though she prefers wine.

Rescheduling many a book club meeting (Apryl Marie Fogel, Lauren Kallus, Clair McLafferty, Monica Aswani) because writing took precedence over reading.

Sharing beer factoids at work (*Birmingham* magazine, Alabama Media Group) whether or not colleagues wanted to hear them.

Stopping by your best friend's house (Apryl Marie Fogel) for a fully cooked dinner and a beer selected by your neighborhood guru (Chandler Busby), if time allows.

Creating lists of things to do after you complete the manuscript, including such glamorous goals as "vacuum."

Commiserating with other authors (Carrie Rollwagen, Kim Cross, Anne Reilly) over beers.

Dropping all pretense of style and hoping that you don't accidentally wear the same outfit twice in a week.

Sending incessant texts to sisters (Cheryl Joy Miner, Cristin Whitley) analyzing every editor suggestion and constant trumpeting of achievements to anyone who will listen (JN315-320, from whom I requested a round of applause after a weekend that generated ten thousand words).

Lifting a glass (likely containing a beverage provided by Allen and Lynn Whitley) to success—past, present and future.

Leaving litter boxes unscooped until a cat (Mac or Harry) complains so loudly that I realize something's wrong.

What was once a lovely Sunday night dinner tradition becoming another text to my boyfriend (Put Ketcham) asking if he would mind another evening of DiGiorno. (He never minds.)

Treading the strange line between introversion and wanting everyone in the world to see what you've done.

To everyone on this list—and the many I surely forgot in my writing-induced haze—thank you.

INTRODUCTION

I won't soon forget my first craft beer experience. Even though I can no longer recall which beer I ordered that night—everything on the menu was a mystery to me—that evening was transformative.

My friend Murray and I were scouting local bars for a *Birmingham* magazine pub-crawl story. The concept was that I'd highlight five tried-and-true favorites and introduce five new hot spots. After catching wind of this venture, a friend insisted I visit the J. Clyde.

Murray and I were in the neighborhood anyway, making a stop at the adjacent martini bar. We poked our heads into the J. Clyde, but we were certain that we were in the wrong place. After a cocktail next door, though, we decided to give it a second chance.

At the time, I was a Bud Light drinker. I had always thought wine and cocktails sounded more sophisticated, but I was somehow more comfortable with a longneck bottle than a martini glass. The flavor of my go-to macro beer wasn't memorable, but it was inoffensive.

The J. Clyde didn't offer Bud Light.

Quickly, I was thrust into a craft beer education. Murray and I returned to the bar many times after that initial April 2007 visit, often sitting at the bar to keep the bartender company. It was there I learned about lambics (I didn't know beer could sparkle like Champagne!) and why stouts tend to be a favorite of craft beer newbies. Bartenders and patrons alike introduced me to Alabama's restrictive beer laws, and I began to wonder how I would ever sip my way through the JC's already extensive

A view of the J. Clyde's back bar in its early days. The space has since been renovated. *Gottfried Kibelka.*

beer list if and when the laws allowed more gourmet-type beers in the local market.

The answer: I wouldn't.

In May 2009, Alabama's alcohol by volume limit increased from 6.0 percent to 13.9. Beer aficionados across the city flocked to the J. Clyde to celebrate. (I was vacationing in Georgia with my mom, but we raised a pair of Chimays to our home state's progress.)

Two years later, the Brewery Modernization Act passed, easing the way for new breweries to open in the state. In May 2012, the legislature again acted to eliminate restrictive consumer laws by allowing larger-sized bottles to be sold in the state. Once again, we saw an increased distribution of beers from elsewhere. A year later, home brewing became legal.

The effect on individuals like me was small in some cases but significant. There's a new brewery on the list at the J. Clyde almost every time I visit, and I'm able to enjoy libations from local breweries and those from far afield no matter where I am in the state. A girlfriend and I often discuss partnering to home brew, and Hops for Honeys offers an outlet to connect with other women while learning about beer.

WE ALMOST DIDN'T GO INTO THE J. CLYDE

I first heard about one of Birmingham's newer nightspots not long after its March opening. Before my visit, a friend insisted that it was a worthwhile nightspot, not just another restaurant. But when I peeked in through the front door, I saw candlelit tables and walls draped in tulle. Nice, but not what I was after.

We left, went next door to the Blue Monkey, but I decided I had to at least give it a shot. Returning, we walked past the dining tables, through a funny jog of a hall and found ourselves deposited at a bar. *This* is what we were looking for.

I selected a beer from a selection creeping toward 200, and then found a table on the covered patio. The J. Clyde is surrounded by other Cobb Lane businesses, creating an atmosphere that is at once cozy and cosmopolitan. We almost didn't go in, but we'll *definitely* go back.

—Carla Jean Whitley, *Birmingham* magazine, July 2007

But the ramifications for the breweries, their employees and the state of Alabama go beyond simple recreation. Craft beer is a rapidly growing industry in the United States; it saw a 20.0 percent dollar sales growth in 2013, even while overall beer sales were down 1.9 percent from the previous year, according to the Brewers Association. Alabama has been quick to jump on board. A couple of former fraternity brothers founded the state's oldest brewery in 2008, and Alabama is home to thirteen such establishments as of this writing. That has meant an increase in business not only for those employees but also for area bars and distributors. Festivals draw people from outside the region, and an established craft beer scene increases quality of life—an important factor for attracting and retaining talent. The Brewers Association indicates that it had a $238.1 million economic impact in 2012—and there's no reason to believe that will drop anytime soon.

The state's beer culture has changed for the better—and it all started in Birmingham.

TIMELINE

S ources offer conflicting reports of when Alabama's first brewery opened, with dates ranging from 1819 to 1874. Regardless, the first brewery in the state was almost certainly not in Birmingham. The dates listed for breweries below generally indicate the date on which the first beer was sold.

1885–1908	Birmingham Brewery becomes the city's first brewery and the first brewery in the state to brew lagers rather than ales.
1887	Birmingham Brewery is renamed Philipp Schillinger Brewing Co.
1889–1893	Birmingham Brewing Co.
1897–1908	Alabama Brewing Co. (continues as an ice manufacturer until 1917).
1907	The Alabama legislature passes a bill allowing counties to vote on going dry. In October, Jefferson County votes to do so.
1908	Jefferson County's prohibition goes into effect on January 1, although breweries have until May 28 to eliminate stock.
1911	In August, Jefferson County votes to go wet.
1915	Statewide prohibition begins in July.
1919	The Volstead Act passes, defining which alcoholic beverages are permissible and which are not. Later in the year, the Eighteenth Amendment makes illegal the production, transport and sale of alcohol.

1920	The Eighteenth Amendment goes into effect on January 17.
1933	The Twenty-first Amendment to the United States Constitution repeals Prohibition on February 21.
1937	Alabama's statewide prohibition ends, and Jefferson County votes wet thereafter.
1992	The Brewpub Act passes, leading to the birth of modern-day brewing in Alabama.
1992–1998	Birmingham Brewing Co.
1993–2004	The Mill Bakery, Eatery and Brewery.
1995–2000	Southside Cellar Brewing Co. Magic City Brewery.
1996–1998	Breckenridge Brewery.
1997–2000	Vulcan Breweries.
1998–2000	Little Star Brewing Co./Mad Monk.
2007–present	The J. Clyde.
2008–present	Good People Brewing Co.
2009	Governor Bob Riley signs the Gourmet Beer Bill into law in May, raising beer's alcohol by volume limit from 6.0 percent to 13.9 percent, matching the limit on wine.
2010	The women's craft beer education group Hops for Honeys forms.
2011	Governor Bentley signs the Brewery Modernization Act, which eliminates the restrictions of taprooms and on-site tastings in Alabama breweries. Taprooms quickly become the norm. Brewpub restrictions are also loosened.
2011–present	Avondale Brewing Co.
2012	The Gourmet Bottle Bill goes into effect in August, allowing the sale of beer in bottles as large as 750 ml, or 25.4 ounces.
2012–present	Hop City Craft Beer and Wine. Cahaba Brewing Co.
2012–2014	Beer Engineers.
2013	On May 9, Alabama becomes the forty-ninth state to legalize home brewing.
2013–present	Trim Tab Brewing Co.

LOCATIONS

Avondale Brewing Co.: 201 Forty-first Street South

Birmingham Brewery (later renamed Phillipp Schillinger Brewing Co.), Birmingham Brewing Co. and Alabama Brewing Co.: Between Twenty-first and Twenty-second Streets South and Avenues D and E, which are now Fourth and Fifth Avenues South

Birmingham Brewing Co.: 3118 Third Avenue South

Breckenridge Brewery: 1908 Eleventh Avenue South

Cahaba Brewing Co.: 2616 Third Avenue South, scheduled to move into 4500 Fifth Avenue South by the end of 2015

Good People Brewing Co.: 114 Fourteenth Street South, started at 1035 Twentieth Street South

Hop City Craft Beer and Wine: 2924 Third Avenue South

The J. Clyde: 1312 Cobb Lane

Little Star Brewing Co./Mad Monk: 3118 Third Avenue South

Magic City Brewery: 420 Twenty-first Street South, across the street from the location of the city's first breweries

Southside Cellar Brewing Co.: 1035 Twentieth Street South

Trim Tab Brewing Co.: 2721 Fifth Avenue South

Vulcan Breweries: 3118 Third Avenue South; contract brewed through Little Star Brewing Co.

World of Beer: 1005 Twentieth Street South

I
EARLY DAYS

First there was Birmingham. Then there was beer.

Wait—let's back up a bit. Six-thousand-year-old Babylonian clay tablets portray brewing—and include recipes. *Mayflower* passenger John Alden, a barrel maker, was responsible for ensuring that the ship's supply of beer didn't rot. The first shipment of beer arrived in Virginia in 1607. Breweries were among the first businesses in what would eventually become the United States.

Beer is an ancient beverage, and just as it was in the colonial United States, the fermented drink was an early concern in Birmingham, Alabama. The city sprung forth in 1871 at the point where the railroad tracks met and the ingredients for steel abounded. Its rapid population growth soon earned Birmingham the moniker "Magic City." That population was thirsty, and so in 1884, Philipp Schillinger opened Birmingham's first brewery.

His effort was part of a national trend; in 1810, the thirty-four-year-old country was home to 140 breweries that accounted for 183,000 barrels of beer per year, according to *The Brewmaster's Table*. By 1873, that number had skyrocketed to 4,131 and 9 million barrels annually.

Schillinger's Birmingham Brewery wasn't the German immigrant's first showing either. Schillinger was a founder of Louisville, Kentucky's Phoenix Brewery in 1865. But he saw Birmingham as a city on the rise and was attracted by its possibility. He arrived in town in 1883 and in 1884 organized Birmingham Brewery. The fledgling operation sold its first beer on April 9, 1885, and continued to grow with the city. It produced eight thousand barrels in its first year and was the first lager brewery in the state.

A billboard advertising Jos. Schlitz Brewing Co. stands in front of a Birmingham apartment building on First Avenue North in the first half of the 1900s. Schlitz was one of the nation's most popular beers. *Birmingham, Alabama Public Library Archives.*

The following year brought plenty of celebration with Schillinger riding the lead float in the city's first Mardi Gras parade on March 8. The float celebrated the king of beer, drinking to the crowd's health, and was drawn by four horses. A second, smaller wagon carried kegs of beer. It was an appropriate celebration for the city's first brewery, which in that year increased its capacity to ten thousand barrels.

Upon incorporating on February 18, 1887, Schillinger renamed the operation Philipp Schillinger Brewing Company. By 1889, its extra pale beer had become the most popular. The company bottled beer especially for family use, and the bottling factory ran night and day to keep up with demand.

Although the brewery's namesake died in 1890, it continued in his stead. Sons August (president and treasurer), Louis (general manager and superintendent) and Colonel Erwin (secretary) continued their father's legacy. The brothers were active in the community, including with organizations such as Birmingham Lodge No. 79, Benevolent and Protective Order of Elks. Based on newspaper articles of the day, their involvement brought high regard to the business. The brewery sat adjacent to a bottling plant and private springs, from which the brewery acquired water for production. An ice factory could produce up to one hundred tons. The total operation filled the block between Twenty-first and Twenty-second Streets and Avenues D and E (today Fourth and Fifth).

For a time, it seemed as though growth potential was limitless. The bottling plant shipped the beer to outside interests, and between 1901 and 1903, Schillinger's capacity doubled to thirty thousand barrels of beer. The thirsty city was, by the late 1890s, home to at least fifty-seven saloons, according to a city directory. Birmingham's population was 38,145.

The Young & Vann Supply Co. Building, located at 1731 First Avenue North, was constructed in 1893 as an Anheuser-Busch distribution center. The industrial supply company for which it is named took residence in 1910, and the building has since housed Wee Care Academy, a number of design-related organizations and Birmingham History Center. It is now home to Alabama Media Group. *Author's collection.*

Alabama Brewing Co. was forced to empty three hundred barrels of beer into the Birmingham streets during Prohibition. *Hunt, O.V.U.S. "Birmingham's Last Brewery" Brantley Collection, Special Collections, Samford University Library, Birmingham. D-000045.*

Birmingham got the reputation of being much like a "wild western mining town with a saloon and brothel on almost every street corner in the downtown area," Malcolm McMillan wrote in *Yesterday's Birmingham*.

As such, perhaps it was predictable that others would attempt to cut themselves a slice of Schillinger's business. On May 27, 1889, W.J. Rushton opened Birmingham Brewing next door to Schillinger. The brewery bought and leased many properties as saloons, where only its beer could be served, a common marketing strategy at the time. In advertisements, the brewery claimed its Erlanger Malt was doctor recommended.

By the early 1890s, however, a coal miners' strike made it difficult for saloon owners to repay the company. Birmingham Brewing was producing seven to eight thousand barrels annually at that point, although it was equipped to brew as many as eighteen thousand barrels of beer annually. The young company declared bankruptcy and went idle. The Rushton family eventually made its fortune through the ice manufacturing business.

The property lay fallow for four years, until New Orleanians Isidore Newmann Sr., Arthur Isnard and A. Cammack invested $60,000 to open Alabama Brewing Co. The company installed new boilers, engines and filters; constructed a two-story bottling house; and added a new thirty-five-ton ice machine for public ice sales. The first beer was brewed in mid-June

1897 and then conditioned for three months before coming to market. The brewery renovations, however, continued for several years.

"He [a *Birmingham News* reporter] felt more like such a brewery belonged to a much larger city. It is a plant Birmingham should well be proud of," a writer declared in an 1897 piece, lauding the brewery's modern equipment. Finer details abounded, with iron pillars marking the brewery entrance and gold lettering announcing its name.

The brewery's cellar was made of iron and cement and featured eighteen casks with plenty of room in which to clean them. Beer was kept in the cellar at freezing temperature for two months. Alabama Iron Works created spiral steps that led from the cellar to a tank room, which housed fourteen tanks of 2,400-gallon capacity. The fermenting room included sixteen tubs. Birmingham Boiler Works created two large boilers, and the American Copper, Brass and Iron Works of Chicago brew kettle was the largest the *Birmingham News* reporter had seen. Whenever possible, materials and equipment were purchased from within Birmingham. Iron pillars supported each room, and the building was labeled fireproof. After discovering natural gas on site while drilling for water in 1899, the brewery incorporated that into its operations.

The brewery ultimately added a seventy-five-ton machine in its adjoining refrigeration plant, and the brewery owners declared it the state's largest ice machine. Capital stock ultimately increased to $220,000. A line of the Birmingham Belt Railroad picked up out-of-town shipments from the plant, which offered both draft and bottled beer. Local deliveries kept twenty to twenty-five teams occupied.

The New Orleans capitalists selected J.L. Knoepfler, a nine-year Anheuser-Busch employee, as ABC's general manager and secretary-treasurer. (Birmingham Gas Company's B.F. Rosen served as president.) Knoepfler oversaw growth that continued alongside renovations, with the company's output increasing from five thousand barrels in 1898 to forty thousand and as many as one hundred employees by 1903.

J.M. Wizen purchased the brewery in the early 1900s, and Dr. Louis Schulhoefer replaced Val Herr as brewmaster. The brewery added a saloon on site, where consumers could enjoy the beer that the *Birmingham News*, in 1909, described as "without a superior for strength, purity and flavor."

Even as Birmingham's beer scene grew, change was on the horizon. In 1848, people began pushing the use of unfermented wine for communion, with some arguing that the original Lord's Supper surely did not use fermented wine. Alabama's first chapter of the Woman's Christian

The Woman's Christian Temperance Union campaigns near a polling place in the early 1900s. *Birmingham, Alabama Public Library Archives.*

Temperance Union (WCTU) was formed in Tuscaloosa in 1881 and quickly became popular among Alabama women. The WCTU originated in Ohio in 1873 and, by 1883, had spread to every state except North Carolina and Mississippi. Members pledged abstinence from alcohol and supported prohibition measures. Men could become honorary members. However, the union divided its efforts to cover a number of issues, including Sunday school work, scientific investigation and others, which slowed its success.

Even with the WCTU's divided focus, other organizations joined the prohibition cause. The Methodist Episcopal Church endorsed temperance in 1880, and in 1886, its general conference recommended occasional Sunday school lessons to support temperance. Prohibitionists first worked against saloons but soon promoted complete abstinence from alcohol.

"I do not believe in the make-believe prohibition that is existing in Alabama. It is leading more boys and men to the devil than anything that has ever occurred," said Honorable E.W. Barrett, editor of the *Birmingham Age-Herald.* The *Birmingham News* and the *Birmingham Ledger,* however, were prohibition papers. *Birmingham News* editor Rufus N. Rhodes worked with Mayor George Ward, the Anti-Saloon League and others to promote prohibition. It was the best way to address the city's problems, which they believed were tied to saloons. The owners of such companies, on the other hand, were eager to get rid of the mayor.

As the prohibition movement gained popularity, breweries took steps to prepare. Schillinger registered the trademark for Beerine, a non-intoxicating temperance beverage, in 1901. It never caught on.

The industry continued to thrive locally through 1907, the state's best year for beer production with 114,967 barrels made. The prohibitionists had their day, though. On February 26, 1907, the Alabama legislature passed a bill that allowed counties to vote on going dry. Jefferson County held its vote on October 28, 1907. On that day, those groups and the WCTU gathered at the courthouse to encourage voters to vote dry.

"The thing came to a vote here, but nobody worried about it. There were 132 saloons in town, and everybody figured each saloon could muster 10 votes to beat it," H.S. Ryan, then city clerk, recalled to the *Birmingham News* in the 1950s.

The majority of Birmingham voted to remain wet, but the rural residents swayed the vote. The measure passed by 1,800 votes, and "Praise God from Whom All Blessings Flow" was sung in the streets during revival meetings. Birmingham was the only major Alabama city to go dry.

Saloons closed on January 1, 1908, but breweries had until May 28 to get rid of their stock. Alabama Brewing Co. was unable to do so, and three hundred barrels of beer met an unfortunate end as they were poured into the street on May 28. The company continued during prohibition as an ice manufacturer, with president Wizen active as vice-president of the twenty-three-member, New Orleans–based Southern Brewers Association. However, in 1917, ABC ceased operation. The building housed an ice plant from 1922 to 1937 and was used for storage thereafter. It was demolished in 1952 and replaced by a parking lot.

Even under countywide prohibition, there was alcohol to be had. Locker clubs allowed people to drink if the alcohol was obtained legally. Only two clubs in Birmingham absolutely upheld prohibition law, according to an article in the December 30, 1909 edition of *Frank Leslie's Weekly*. The same article indicated that nine out of ten juries wouldn't convict during Jefferson County prohibition. "You can get whiskey in Birmingham today with as much ease as you can in New York," it read.

Meanwhile, the nation hit a new record. In 1911, the United States produced the most beer per capita in the world, with 62.8 million barrels, equaling twenty-one gallons, per capita. Jefferson County veered back toward national trends on August 24 of that year, voting to go wet. Nine states had gone dry by 1912, but in Birmingham, rumors of a 100,000-barrel operation by J.F. Donahoo circulated. Imperial City Brewing was said to have $500,000 in capital, but money isn't everything. On July 1, 1915, Alabama's statewide prohibition began. The massive brewery was never to be.

The prohibitionists continued to have their way. In 1919, the Volstead Act passed as a precursor to the Eighteenth Amendment, a result of fervent Protestants who wanted to reduce crime and alcohol consumption. The Volstead Act defined what beverages were off limits (medical usage remained acceptable, for example) and detailed punishments, while the Eighteenth Amendment actually outlawed production, transportation and sale of alcohol. National Prohibition went into effect in 1920.

The country remained dry until February 21, 1933, when the Twenty-first Amendment brought the Prohibition experiment to an end. *Beer for Dummies* notes that, per government statistics, Prohibition cost the United States an excess of $34.5 billion in lost tax revenue and enforcement costs.

After thirteen years of national Prohibition, tastes had changed. Sodas grew in popularity during that time, creating a competitive industry. Brewers dumbed down the beer to make it easier to drink, matching the palate soda had developed.

Laws prohibited alcohol by volume greater than 4 percent, according to *The Brewmaster's Table*, limiting brewers in what they could produce. There was also pressure to keep costs low during the Great Depression, so adjunct ingredients such as rice and corn, which were cheaper than barley malt and already being incorporated by bootleggers, were introduced. Thus, the American macro-brewed lager became the country's standard beer.

"Before prohibition, beer was local. There were those who had the foresight to get into distributing other products like ice cream, and those were able to weather the storm. Most did not though. That left the country with only a few major distributors," Birmingham Beverage owner Harry Kampakis said eighty years later to the *Birmingham Business Journal*.

Tastes weren't the only way Alabama breweries were affected. The tied-house system was the norm before Prohibition, allowing breweries to own local saloons in which only that brewery's beers were available. After Prohibition, however, the three-tier system became standard. That outlawed any single individual—or a relative of such—owning the brewer, the distributor and the retailer. Canning, introduced in 1935, created an additional challenge. Breweries that couldn't afford canning equipment were at a further disadvantage. About four hundred American breweries reopened after Prohibition, but about half eventually closed because of financial challenges.

Although national Prohibition had ended, the state did not act quickly. Some Birmingham residents were drinking openly—but illegally—by 1937 and were even pictured on the cover of *Alabama* magazine, beers in hand. The Alabama legislature eventually returned to the local option in 1937, ending the statewide alcohol ban. Birmingham remained wet thereafter.

In fact, some later protests had an unexpected effect on alcohol sales. In June 1945, the state legislature was again considering liquor-related bills, and people picketed at three Birmingham locations of state liquor stores. A woman dressed in a devil costume, carrying a pitchfork and a sign that read, "I am well pleased in what you are doing," depicting a bottle marked XXX and signed, "The Devil." She told police she was a member of Avondale Baptist Church but didn't reveal her name. Crowds gathered at the scene, and stores reported that liquor sales increased.

While sales may have been up, production continued to shift. In 1950, there were 407 breweries in operation. Between 1949 and 1958, 185 breweries closed or were sold nationwide. By 1983, fifty-one owners operated 80 breweries. The top six—Anheuser-Busch, Miller, Heinemann, Stroh, Coors and Pabst—controlled 92 percent of the country's beer production. Local beer was largely a thing of the past.

2

THE BREWPUB ERA

After a long drought, the Brewpub Act of 1992 again introduced brewing to Alabama. However, the restrictions were plentiful: A brewpub must be located in a historic building or site in a wet county and/or wet municipality in which beer was brewed for the public prior to Prohibition. The brewpub could not sell or distribute beer off site, and it must also include a restaurant with a capacity of at least eighty. The brewpub was restricted to brewing ten thousand barrels or fewer per year.

The act's passage left Georgia and Mississippi as the only states outlawing brewpubs. It also left a distinction between microbreweries and brewpubs. The former could sell its product only in bottles or kegs, either of which must run through an outside distributor. A brewpub could sell it in its bar and restaurant but couldn't bottle it.

Although Alabama was late to the game, the changes were evidence of a growing trend. According to *Beer for Dummies*, interest in microbreweries began in 1977, when New Albion Brewing opened in Sonoma, California. In 1980, the United States was home to four microbreweries and no brewpubs. Growth was rapid. In 1993, 350 brewpubs existed nationally; the Mobile *Press-Register* reported that they were concentrated in the Pacific Northwest, and each produced no more than fifteen thousand barrels annually. By 1996, reports showed that the country was home to 900 brewpubs and 900 microbreweries. The Association of Brewers estimated that microbrewery sales doubled every year between 1986 and 1994; however, Prohibition-era laws held back such growth in the South.

The Mill and Southside Cellar

With the passage of the Brewpub Act, Birmingham's tastes began to shift. The Mill Bakery, Eatery and Brewery opened in Birmingham's Five Points South neighborhood in 1993. The eatery, which also had a Huntsville location, served contract-brewed beers, although the owners expressed interest in brewing beer themselves. The plan was to open a brewery in the basement of the Pickwick Plaza space, but regulators couldn't be convinced that the two were separate businesses and would not approve it.

"It is so political, bureaucratic craziness," owner Jeff Blomeyer said to the *Anniston Star.*

Ultimately, Southside Cellar opened with a pane of glass separating it from the restaurant. Its grand opening was set for November 18, 1995.

"It's a return to the status quo that existed before Prohibition," brewmaster John Kater said.

Kater's existence was itself reason for excitement; a 1996 *Birmingham News* article reported that he was only one of about a dozen brew masters in the world to have completed the University of California–Davis's master's program in fermentation science. At the time, it was the only such program in existence.

"He's kind of the Willy Wonka of beer in Birmingham," 1996 Birmingham Brewfest coordinator G. Steven Godsey said to the *News.*

Kater, who lectured at the beer festival, and Southside Cellar saw success with the beer. It was distributed to several area eateries, including Cellar Beer Garden, located in the same shopping center beneath Cosmos Pizza. The brewery's Ship in a Bottle Oatmeal Stout medaled at the World Beer Championships in 1997, and Meaning of Life Pensive Red Ale took home a bronze medal in 1998.

Birmingham Brewing

City Stages, a Birmingham music festival, often introduced concertgoers to new bands, new songs and new experiences. And in 1992, the event also introduced new beer.

Birmingham Brewing Co. (BBC) began brewing its Red Mountain beers in May and debuted seventy-four kegs at the three-day June music festival. The beer sold out. In August, the brewery began distributing its wares in bottles.

Birmingham Brewing Co. was located on Third Avenue South in the midst of an industrial area. *Steve Betts.*

The 6,500-square-foot microbrewery was the first in Alabama in decades (the first in the Deep South was located in Louisiana). By 1993, Birmingham Brewing employed three full-time brewery employees, two part-time and two full-time in marketing. They worked together in support of the brewery's simply named beers—red ale, golden ale, golden lager and golden wheat—distributed in Alabama and parts of Mississippi, Georgia and Florida. Six-packs sold for about six dollars.

The brewery, located in an industrial section of Third Avenue South, wasn't much to look at. "It's an area filled with ugly but functional buildings for electronics firms, trucking companies, paint and body shops and distributors," David Tortorano wrote in the *Press-Register*.

Brewer and musician Lee Nicholson, attorney R. Ben Hogan and investors purchased the space and got to brewing. By 1993, Nicholson was gone and John Zanteson was brewmaster. He began home brewing while enrolled at California's Humboldt State University and went on to work at a brewpub in the state. Like many microbrewers, he shunned the use of additives and pasteurization and opted for less filtration. The result was heavier hops and malt and a beer with a shelf life of about three months.

Sales increased 30 percent between January 1993 and January 1994, bringing the brewery to its break-even point, which Hogan indicated they were happy to reach so early.

The brewery expanded its storage in March 1994, increasing capacity to 7,500 barrels. Birmingham Brewing distributed throughout the Southeast, with clients in Washington, D.C., as well. "We sold more beer in Athens, Georgia, than we did here," recalled Steve Betts, who came to BBC as production manager and eventually brewer after fifteen years with Miller. "That was a good thing, but it was a strange phenomenon. Why make it here and ship it all the way there? The middle men involved and everything eats your profit up," he said.

The company's ten-year plan was to market 80 percent of its beer in Birmingham. Despite success, that didn't come to pass.

In 1995, BBC was listed among America's best brewers, according to a New Hampshire group. Red Mountain Red Ale brought home a silver medal from the 1995 World Beer Championships and an honorable mention from the 1995 Great American Beer Festival Awards. Its Red Mountain Ale built a particular following among women, brewer Mickey Stringer told the *Birmingham News*, and when he visited, *Simon and Schuster Pocket Guide to Beer* author Michael Jackson spoke kindly of the wares.

The brewery began to experiment with additional beers in the mid-'90s, introducing a dark lager for the Christmas season in 1995 and Red Mountain Bock in 1996. It was available on draft only and was the first beer that was Betts's idea from start to finish.

From 1992 to 1996, the brewery averaged five thousand barrels annually. Average annual sales exceeded $400,000, and Ben Hogan told the *Birmingham News* that he hadn't had many hangovers in the past year—an important note, the paper observed, because it underscored the fact that the craft brewery movement is about quality, not drunkenness.

But the landscape soon changed. In August 1996, around the time Betts left for an Ohio brewery, Hogan listed the business for sale. "We have been an artistic success, but the demands of my law practice do not allow me to do justice to the business side of this brewery. I hope to find new owners who will develop the tradition and carry it into the next century," he said to the *Birmingham News*. Hogan had announced earlier in the year that he'd like to sell for $1.2 million, but when an investor group stepped up, terms of the sale weren't disclosed.

Brad Fournier, who in 1996 left Magic City for Birmingham Brewing, remained at the brewery after investor group BBC Acquisition Co., formed by LBI Investments, acquired it. Spokesman Lee Busby said the brewery's potential was impressive, and he was interested in exploring private-label options.

CRAFT BEER EDUCATION

That change continued outside of pub walls. In the fall of 1994, Tom Lamb taught a University of Alabama at Birmingham special studies class titled "The Fine Art of Beer Tasting." The adult education program took place during three September nights and included tastings and a tour of Birmingham Brewing Co. for fifty-five dollars' tuition. The class filled so quickly that Lamb opened a second session in October.

"It's not particularly sitting around on a Saturday night swilling beer and watching football anymore," he said to the *Birmingham News*.

By 1995, craft beer represented a rapidly growing segment of the national beer market. Although light beers retained 35 percent market share, craft grew as much as 40 percent annually for three consecutive years, and in 1994, it grew by 50 percent, according to an article in the *New Brewer*.

The influence wasn't limited to microbreweries. In the mid-'90s, Anheuser-Busch introduced Faust, Black & Tan, Muenchener, Elephant Red and Carlsberg in Alabama. A marketing consultant for Birmingham Budweiser told the *Birmingham Post-Herald* that Birmingham was the third city to receive the beers because of its specialty sales. The brands had previously been sold in Alabama in the early 1900s but were discontinued during Prohibition.

A 1996 article in the *Birmingham News* highlighted the popularity of wine dinners bookended by beer tastings to start and fine cigars as the conclusion.

MAGIC CITY BREWERY

In March 1995, the 400 block of what is now Richard Arrington Junior Boulevard again served as Mesopotamia for Birmingham beer. The first Birmingham brewpub to successfully clear the Brewpub Act's hoops was Magic City Brewery, which opened in the Weldon Martin Building, across the street from where Philipp Schillinger, Alabama Brewing and Birmingham Brewing sat a century earlier. The historic warehouse was constructed in 1920 for Weldon Martin Rubber and housed a number of automotive businesses through the years. In 1991, the area, identified as the Automotive Historic District, was listed on the National Register of Historic Places.

"We often talk about what Birmingham has lost. What this makes possible is the return of something that was here, although in a different form, more

Merienda now sits in the building once occupied by Magic City Brewery. *Author's collection.*

than 100 years ago," Birmingham Public Library archivist Marvin Whiting said to the *Birmingham News* upon the brewpub's opening.

The $1 million Magic City Brewery was the second Alabama brewpub owned and operated by City Brewing Investment Corporation, which had already seen success by opening Mobile's Port City Brewery in 1993. Brewpubs were at this time opening at a rate of one daily, based on information from the Association of Brewers.

Magic City occupied nine thousand square feet in the former Tom Williams Dodge showroom. A glass-enclosed brewery stood center stage with eleven five-hundred-gallon tanks, surrounded by the bar and requisite restaurant. Owner Sam Casto had hoped to open earlier, but Alabama law required equipment to be in place and ready to go before a brewery could get a license from the federal Bureau of Alcohol, Tobacco and Firearms; that must be followed by Alabama Beverage Control and then final issues with the city.

"We think this is another amenity for the area," Michael Calvert, executive director of economic development organization Operation New Birmingham, said to the *Birmingham News* prior to opening.

The brewpub launched a founder's club, whose members were invited to pre-opening parties on March 8 and 9, prior to the public opening on March 10. The members, who paid a fee of $100 to join, were to be listed on a plaque above the bar and received T-shirts, hats and invitations to future events. They were the only customers allowed to make reservations. (Early on, two-hour waits were routine, as demand outweighed supply.)

A *Birmingham Post-Herald* article indicated that the brewpub pulled in $85,000 a week upon opening, attracting drinkers and diners alike with specials such as a malted barley shake made with fat-free yogurt and a splash of Old Oxmoor Stout beer.

Don Alan Hankins, who had previously worked at Birmingham Brewing, came on board as head brewer. "I said, 'I'll scrub your tanks. I'll wash your floors. I'll do it all for free.' I did it for about three months, and they knew I was serious," he recalled to the *Huntsville Times*. Within a year, he was in the Magic City position but soon longed to return to his roots in Huntsville. Hankins planned to open a brewpub in the Rocket City in 1996, but Alabama's restrictive laws and California-based parent company CBIC's interests elsewhere delayed Hankins's plans. (He ultimately opened Huntsville's Olde Towne Brewing Co. in 2004.)

Brad Fournier followed as brewmaster, moving to Birmingham from Mobile, where he had been part of Port City. Fournier trained at the University of California–Davis's fermentation program and at the Institute of Brewing in London. "He was a good brewer. He was a good formulator," said BBC's Betts, whom Fournier eventually succeeded. He developed Magic City's Electra Light, Schillinger's Star, Old Oxmoor Stout and Sloss Steamer, all year-round beers. Reds became big business in the mid-'90s, and Sloss Steamer, a special bitter, sold well. Fournier described it as a halfway point between traditional American macros and European-style beers.

Although Birmingham Brewing Co. was already established a mile away, Fournier was quick to say that the two companies were not in competition.

"As far as our industry is concerned, places like Red Mountain and places like ours help foster each other," he told the *Birmingham News*. "Before Prohibition, breweries like this were all over the nation. Prohibition nailed all of them."

Owner Sam Casto elaborated: "Each one of these brewpubs are offering a product that you can't get anywhere else in the city. You can get chicken fingers at any restaurant in town, but you can't buy our beer but right here."

But when Birmingham Brewing Co. went on the market in 1996, it had an unexpected effect on Magic City's business: people confused the two and assumed Magic City was preparing to close. Julie Dekle, marketing manager for City Brewery Investment Corporation, said sales dropped 20 percent, accounting for a loss of $5,000 a week.

However, as trends shifted, Magic City ultimately saw business changing, with additions such as martini and cigar menus in the spotlight by 1999. It closed on June 16, 2000, one month after its fifth anniversary. General manager Rick Odom indicated that the decision was made by the corporate office in California. "We were a restaurant trying to survive as a brewery, and I don't think just being a brewery is going to survive here," he told the *Birmingham News*. Marketing was an issue, he said, and the Mill did a much better job of that. Magic City's merchandise marketing wasn't strong, nor was nighttime business. Port City continued as the company's other Alabama interest, marketing and repositioning itself, but it ultimately closed in 2001.

BRECKENRIDGE BREWERY

The city's second brewpub opened in December 1996, one block away from Southside Cellar and the Mill in what is now a Jim 'n' Nick's Bar-B-Q. Richard Squire opened the original brewery in Colorado, and locations in Denver, Buffalo, New York and Dallas preceded Birmingham. The brewery utilized many of its brews in cooking, as well, and other dishes incorporated spent-grain beer bread.

The $2 million microbrewery could produce up to three thousand barrels of beer and included a 250-seat dining room. Ten fermenters lined one wall, and seven tanks and kettles were perched above the bar. Yeast and grain were incorporated into the décor, which also featured wood floors and exposed brick. The ales could take fifteen days to brew, and lagers as long as five months, and the *Birmingham News* dubbed the results a success. Offerings included Avalanche Amber, Mountain Wheat, IPA, oatmeal stout and two seasonal beers, such as Five Points Red or brown nut ale. The paper's reviewer identified the amber as a "hands-down favorite" and noted that the food was also impressive. Everything was made from scratch on site, and there was no freezer on the premises.

Even so, the operation closed in 1998. Kyle Craig, at the Colorado headquarters, said the Birmingham brewpub wasn't profitable and was challenged by high overhead, and they didn't manage it as well as possible. By the time of the location's closing, Breckenridge was up to three Colorado brewpubs and one each in Tennessee, Arizona and Nevada. Buffalo's Breckenridge had also closed.

Vulcan Breweries

Rights to Red Mountain brands passed to Vulcan Breweries in 1996, but the business, which brewed by contract, focused on its own brands. Even before beer hit the market, in August 1997, Vulcan Breweries launched the state's first cyber stock sale. Shares were $1.85 each, with a one-hundred-share minimum purchase. The company hoped to sell $1.2 million worth to finance expansion and marketing.

"It delights me to see little 12-ounce marketing platforms rolling off the line," Vulcan president Lee Busby said to the *Birmingham News* as the company prepared beer bottle labels listing stock option information.

The beer debuted a week after the stock, launching with a pair of free tastings in 1997, offering its lager-style Vulcan Beer at Dave's Pub and its hefeweizen at Dugan's. Both were well received.

"It's easy to drink and I'm definitely pro-Birmingham. If it's something from Birmingham, I'm going to support it," John Feiraby, a customer at the Dave's tasting, told the *Birmingham Post-Herald*.

The company's initial goal was to sell two thousand bottle cases a month and one hundred kegs a month. With a capacity of 11,000 barrels, Vulcan expected to hit 5,500 within a year of its debut.

"I think we've made this beer easy enough to drink that it should be successful with males and females. We definitely like the idea of a crowd of professional women enjoying our beer," Vulcan sales and marketing director Brett Gibson said to the *Post-Herald*.

Success continued for a time, with the hefeweizen taking home bronze from 1997's Great American Beer Festival, in which it competed with eighty-three beers. But when Little Star bought the old Birmingham Brewing facility, owners of each brewing company struggled to agree on terms. Busby said he began looking for an out-of-state contract brewer before the two eventually reestablished their relationship. He estimated a loss of $189,000 in 1998.

The beer became scarce in early 1999 but returned with a vengeance that summer. It was paired with a marketing campaign, conceived by Birmingham Beverage's Harry Kampakis, that included a dollar-per-case donation to restoring the iconic statue at Vulcan Park and Museum. The park had temporarily closed because of the iconic statue's disrepair.

Little Star and Mad Monk

Little Star Brewing Co. purchased the Birmingham Brewing Co. space in 1998. In addition to contract brewing for Vulcan Breweries, Little Star purchased the Mad Monk brands from the Cincinnati-based Mad Monk Beer Co., which had been contract brewing them through a Minnesota brewery. Little Star moved operations to Birmingham and also purchased brands from Miami's Firehouse Brewing Co.

The four Mad Monk beers—Nut Brown Ale, pale ale, pilsner and Rasputin Abbey Ale—were distributed in Birmingham but also far beyond.

"You can't make a living in Alabama with a brewery. We've got it out to five different states, but you've got to be supported by the local market, and they're not going to support it here," Little Star president Marc Anthony said to the *Birmingham News*. "The people are not interested in Alabama right now. It's a Bud, Miller and Coors market. There's not enough demand for it [craft-brewed beer]."

The family operation, which saw Anthony's wife and mother-in-law involved, identified diversification as a key component of its business plan. But Birmingham microbreweries were on the downswing. By 2000, each brewery had ceased producing beer, and the Mill brought in its beer from Pittsburgh.

The building that once housed Birmingham Brewing Co., Vulcan Breweries, Little Star Brewing and Mad Monk Brewing is again more industrial in nature. *Author's collection.*

Little Star was the last of the 1990s Birmingham breweries to close in July 2000. Investors in South Carolina bought the operation and moved it to Greenville.

"We put the seeds out. They started sprouting a little bit. Then when it was gone, people said, 'Where did it go?' I think it could have continued here," said Birmingham Brewing's Steve Betts, who was the last person to brew on Little Star's equipment before it moved to South Carolina. Hogan asked Betts to demonstrate the equipment for the buyers.

But the market wasn't yet ready. Although craft beer was on the rise, the demand in Alabama wasn't enough to sustain the breweries, and the breweries weren't large enough to create the demand on their own, Betts said. Birmingham Brewing, for example, sold as much or more beer in Athens, Georgia, as it did in its namesake city.

"If you can sell it on tap here, that's where you're going to make your biggest profit. You don't have the expense of putting it in a bottle, buying a bottle, all that peripheral stuff," Betts explained. The brewery distributed a significant amount of beer out-of-state. But without a marketing budget to introduce consumers to the beer, it often sat in stores beyond its shelf life. "The beers were good. They were great when they left the brewery, but by the time they got in our peripheral markets, by the time they got to some of the consumers, it was old beer."

The efforts of the '90s brewers weren't enough. Birmingham's brewpub era was over.

3
FREE THE HOPS

Birmingham, the state's largest city, was for years without a beer to call its own. Signs of life remained in other parts of the state—Mr. Jim Cannon's Brewpub in Mobile, Olde Towne Brewing Co. in Huntsville, Old Auburn Ale House and Montgomery Brewpub in their respective cities. But the challenges that plagued the brewpubs and breweries of the '90s remained.

Until one man decided he must do something about that.

It wasn't exactly an epiphany—perhaps more of a gradual dawning—that led Danner Kline to create the grass-roots lobbying organization Free the Hops.

Kline graduated in 2000 from conservative Samford University in Birmingham, and he wasn't much of a partier. But an appreciation for interesting food and drink sent him exploring the limited selection of beer in his neighborhood grocery store. First, Yuengling Traditional Lager drew his attention, and then the brewery's Black and Tan. By 2004, craft beers he sampled in other states had piqued Kline's interest. When he returned home, he realized those beers were not only unavailable, but they were also illegal. Alabama limited beer to 6 percent alcohol by volume and a maximum container size of sixteen ounces. That eliminated more than one-third of beers brewed from being served in Alabama, Kline told *Birmingham Weekly*.

Something had to change.

Kline was then enrolled part time at the Birmingham School of Law, and he thought, "Maybe after law school, I'll do something about this." But his patience quickly wore thin.

"With each passing day, it pissed me off more and more. I'm not real patient when it comes to waiting for something that I'm looking forward to," he recalled. And so, he again turned to the Internet to learn about what had been done before. Were other state's laws so restrictive? Was anyone in Alabama already lobbying to change the laws?

The answers: kind of and no. A handful of other states limited alcohol by volume in beer to 6 percent, but none seemed to have the particular limitations that faced Alabama. In the Yellowhammer State, beer couldn't be sold in a package larger than sixteen ounces, breweries couldn't sell beer on site, brewpubs must be located in historic buildings in counties that brewed beer before Prohibition and home brewing beer was illegal.

While Kline was deep in research, Georgians for World-Class Beer successfully changed that state's ABV law. "The state right next to us just succeeded in making this change. We have a similar culture. There's a lot of parallels between Alabama and Georgia," Kline said.

Meanwhile, North Carolina's Pop the Cap was working on a similar project. The organization started with a group of thirty-five people eager to increase the state's ABV restriction. Kline spoke at length with the organization's Sean Wilson, who shared details of what was involved, strategies, how many hours he invested in the effort and more. Wilson allowed Kline to borrow verbiage from Pop the Cap's site, adapting it to Alabama and launching a website to help find others who liked good beer. (As of 2013, North Carolina was home to ninety-one craft breweries, ranking ninth in the nation.)

"I was just trying to find some small group to help kick things off because at that point I didn't know anybody," Kline recalled. His boss at the time was even a teetotaler. "I didn't really have a base of people to work with."

Kline's interest in home brewing was also developing, and he mentioned the newfound group to Kim Thompson at Alabrew, a home brewing supply store. Thompson included a blurb about the fledgling group in his next customer e-mail, along with Kline's contact information.

Lee Winnige responded to that ad and met with Danner at On Tap Sports Café in Lakeview to talk through the ideas. "Lee has been a barfly—a craft-beer drinking barfly—for a very long time, so he had that base of friends who would be interested that I didn't have," Kline explained. Winnige quickly became vice-president and invited others to the group. With interest established, Free the Hops commenced monthly meetings.

A media onslaught began with an April 7, 2005 piece in *Birmingham Weekly*. Kline and those who came after him have maintained that Free the Hops has never been about making it easier for people to get drunk. Rather, the goal was consistent laws for all types of alcohol. Wine and liquor weren't subject to the same laws, so why should beer be?

"This is because we like good beer and because we want Alabama to have a better reputation," Kline told the paper.

Several members joined in response to the article, and a *Birmingham News* piece followed. Still more people joined, and then ABC 33/40 filmed a segment. "It was just kind of one of those things that builds and builds and builds and builds. We went from a dozen members to a couple hundred members in a few months," Kline said.

(At least one later president of the organization, Gabe Harris, joined based on media coverage: "Why does Alabama not have good beer like other states do? How can I do a little bitty piece of that and help change Alabama for the better? It's my home state; I love Alabama, and I want it to be better. Beer is something that everybody…it's an easy thing to get excited about and want to see Alabama get good beer.")

Free the Hops held several cookouts and similar events to promote interest during the organization's early days. *Gottfried Kibelka.*

Free the Hops held gatherings at downtown and Southside bars to generate interest. At first, the organization focused on recruitment and education before beginning to lobby for change.

But the magic moment was yet to arrive. Shortly after Kline filed incorporation documents, he and Winnige received an e-mail from distributor Birmingham Beverage's Harry Kampakis.

Kampakis had long been interested in an increased ABV law, as it would open up the availability of new beers to distribute. "It's backwards. It's ridiculous. There are so many beers that we can't get here, but I can go buy pure-grain alcohol at a state [ABC] store?" Kampakis lamented to *Birmingham Weekly*.

Over a lunch at Bottega, Kampakis offered Kline and Winnige his business for meetings, his contacts and some financial resources. Kampakis ultimately introduced the pair to Michael Sullivan, a lobbyist who had worked previously on wholesale beer legislation.

"[Harry] was an early believer in Free the Hops, and he saw the potential more so than any other distributor in the state. Harry saw where it was going; he believed in it and felt that was where beer was going," Harris said. "He was the first corporate supporter of Free the Hops and was a huge part of getting us off the ground and where we are now. I give Harry a lot of credit for seeing where beer in general is going. He was right."

Birmingham Brewing Co.'s Steve Betts said he believed Kampakis's interest was born in part out of a desire to own a brewery, but the three-tier system wouldn't allow an individual to own both a distributor and a brewery. "That doesn't mean you can't foster the movement. He did everything he could to foster it," Betts said. "That's good for him. That's good for Alabama. That's good for all of the microbreweries that are here."

It would also affect other businesses, such as retail stores, and offer widespread economic influence. Vulcan Beverages owner Mark Green carried 250 varieties at the time of Free the Hops's formation but told *Birmingham Weekly* he could carry about three thousand beers if the Gourmet Beer and Gourmet Bottle laws passed. He didn't even drink beer—never had a sip. "My customers are dying to get better, high-end beer. I've passed out hundreds of flyers [about Free the Hops] and I've never had anyone hand it back. They just want more choices."

"Really, there's all this wine snobbery that's encouraged, but beer is just seen as a cheap, blue-collar beverage for getting drunk on the weekend. I want to change that image of beer," Kline said to the *Birmingham Weekly*.

Gabe Harris celebrates after winning a bottle of Three Floyds' Dark Lord Imperial Stout during Free the Hops's 2008 holiday party. *Gottfried Kibelka.*

But before the organization could do that, it had to establish an agenda. "Beer culture is a jigsaw puzzle," second Free the Hops president Stuart Carter said to *Birmingham* magazine. Retail sales, brewpubs and breweries, home brewing and container size are all pieces that add up to the larger picture. Each of those factors was considered before Free the Hops determined its priorities.

Although both alcohol by volume limits and container size were immediate concerns, the group decided that taking on the restrictions one at a time seemed more feasible. Because of its wide-reaching effects, the ABV limit came first.

"Of those, the ABV limitation was having a much bigger impact than the container. We were going to get a lot more benefit more quickly than changing the container size," Kline said.

Presenting these restrictions as an economic issue would be key, Kline and Kampakis believed. Kampakis's involvement was directly related to that; he could present the issue to the Wholesalers Association, a group that would see direct financial gain as a result of the proposed changes.

"A lot of these specialty microbrewers just don't have the capacity to go after every market in the United States even if they could," Winnige said to the *Birmingham Weekly*. "They're not going to choose a state that only allows them to

Since the inaugural event in 2007, Sloss Furnaces has served as the site for Magic City Brewfest. *Gabe Harris.*

sell one of their beers…It's just not worth the paperwork, the limitations and the hassle. So that means a lot of the beers we're missing out on aren't even illegal. These are four or five percent [alcohol by volume] beers that we don't get." New Belgium's Fat Tire, for example, was long touted by Alabama beer fans as a beer they'd love to have but couldn't. New Belgium didn't distribute in the state until 2014 or in the South until 2008. The amber Fat Tire is 5.2 percent.

Kampakis proposed taking legislators to a beer dinner in Atlanta to underscore the differences. "When it's over, I'll show them the tab. And I'll say, 'Here's all the beer, and the revenue, you're missing. We should be entertaining you in Alabama and spending all this money,'" he said to the *Birmingham Weekly.*

"We're not promoting alcohol; we're promoting consistency in the law," Danner Kline told the *Huntsville Times.* That mantra showed up in a variety of media. "It will improve the image of the state, making us a more desirable tourist destination, and it will also, I believe, increase tax revenue," Kline said to Comedy Central's *The Daily Show.* The 2005 segment poked fun at Alabama for its conservative ways—including footage from Cullman's dry Oktoberfest—as well as Kline himself and his intense love of beer. In 2007, though, Free the Hops launched Magic City Brewfest, spreading the love with an educational and fundraising effort that has drawn more breweries to the typically sold-out event each year.

The J. Clyde's menu features grass-fed meat and locally sourced ingredients whenever possible. *Brent Boyd.*

The year 2007 brought another milestone: the opening of the J. Clyde. The restaurant and pub offered another opportunity to educate consumers; Free the Hops had previously set up an information table at bars—without great success. "That was a fairly low effectiveness rate because when people are going out drinking, they don't want to stop at an information table and talk about much of anything," Kline recalled with a laugh. But by emphasizing craft beer and including table talkers and other materials, the J. Clyde helped reinforce Free the Hops's message.

Co-owner Jerry Hartley, who opened the pub alongside siblings Bryan and Susan, spent time living in Germany and developing an affinity for European-style beers. Within its first year of operation, the restaurant added cask beer, which is naturally carbonated, stored in kegs and dispensed through beer engines. Hartley purchased his own firkins and shipped them to breweries willing to fill them; they would then return the firkins via distributors.

"Cask beer allows the brewer to stretch beyond the basic theme of the brewery's stock products, much as improvisation allows musicians to take a song in many different directions," Eric Velasco wrote in the *Birmingham News*. Brewers can add ingredients to beer destined for a cask, so it will continue to develop as it ferments in the cask. "With the way beer evolves, when you drink a cask ale you will never be able to get that exact flavor again," Hartley told the *Birmingham News*.

As the state's beer movement solidified, the J. Clyde grew. It now boasts sixty taps, 125 bottles and twenty bombers available at any time. Thirteen taps are dedicated to Alabama beers. "When I put up those 13 taps in April 2012, I thought that would be enough for 20 years. Within a year, we ran out of room. We had every brewery in Alabama. It's amazing to see the growth," Hartley said to *Birmingham* magazine.

The J. Clyde was home to the city's first Randall, which allows beer to be filtered through additives such as fresh hops or coffee. Its food is locally sourced whenever possible and seasonal.

"No restaurant or retailer has been bigger for the growth of craft beer in Birmingham than the J. Clyde has been," Free the Hops's Gabe Harris said.

"Reforming Alabama's beer law will change Alabama's perception in the international community," Carter, a Scot, said to *Birmingham* magazine. And Free the Hops was determined to make it so.

4
GOOD PEOPLE BREWING CO.

In the early days of Free the Hops, Gabe Harris would often announce at meetings, "'Somebody's going to start a brewery. They're going to start one. It's going to be called Good People. And I know them.' No one believed me," Harris recalled.

Those "somebodies" were Eric Schultenover, Jason Malone and Michael Sellers, the latter the husband of Harris's childhood friend Melinda. When the gates opened for the first Magic City Brewfest in 2007, a sandwich-board sign announcing Good People Beer Co. was prominently displayed. "I told y'all," said Harris, who is himself now an owner of Fairhope Brewing in south Alabama.

Jason Malone and Michael Sellers met at Auburn University, where they were members of Sigma Chi. But at the time, the duo was far from becoming the beer lovers they are today. "It was more of the beer-drinking experience from a social standpoint, party standpoint, event standpoint than it was the actual quality of the liquid," Malone said.

Malone's introduction to craft beer came while in school for his master's of business administration, during which time he traveled to Ireland. Malone began training himself for Irish beer by consuming Guinness while stateside. While overseas, he continued drinking Guinness and developed a taste for it, as well as English-style ales that he hadn't previously tried. "Good beer is like good wine, good food, anything like that. Once you've had good, it's hard to go back," he said.

Good People Brewing Co.'s logo features a vintage-style yellow pickup truck. *Paul MacWilliams.*

Before long, Malone realized he could brew his own beer: "I thought you had to be a huge factory in some unknown place and it just magically appeared on the shelf." He took up the hobby in the early 2000s.

Meanwhile, Sellers was on his own craft-beer journey. Southside Cellar's Meaning of Life Pensive Red Ale, with its eight malts and four types of hops, grabbed his attention during a meal at the Mill, a restaurant adjacent to that brewery. His next a-ha moment, like Malone's, came overseas. While traveling for work in Australia, Sellers encountered Little Creatures Pale Ale, which became his go-to beer in the country.

When Sellers returned to America, he discovered his old friend was walking the same path. The pair began brewing at home and together, traveling the miles between Nashville, where Malone lived, and Birmingham, where Sellers had set up residence. At first, they had no dreams of brewing professionally. Malone's career as a financial consultant, and Sellers's in software sales, was moving along just fine. But around 2007, the buddies began to daydream.

"When you make beer, it's a product of sharing. You don't make beer and sit in your basement drinking it by yourself. You make beer and hang out with people and drink it with people, and they give you their feedback on it," Malone said.

"All these things are incremental moments, doors to get you to take the leap of faith to go past the home brewing stage," Sellers said.

As they began to form the business, the duo struggled with the name. "We wanted to capture the South, but we didn't want it to be too 'ducks with bonnets.' We didn't want it to be too kitschy, but we wanted to encompass the newer South," Sellers explained. The perfect name came while Sellers was at an office Christmas party with his then girlfriend, now wife, Melinda. One of Melinda's colleagues was identifying people at the party, giving Sellers background on each. "He's like, 'That's Jim, he's good people…' I thought, 'This would be great.' It just clicked off the bat," Sellers said. Melinda's mom drafted the logo with an old pickup truck, again trying to capture the spirit of the region without going too far afield.

Once the pair decided to go into business, there was no question about where: Birmingham was it. Malone was born in the city and attended college two hours away, and Sellers was already in the city, which at the time was without a brewery. With the defunct Southside Cellar Brewing on their minds, they had a plan.

"We thought it would be really easy: hey, let's go down and buy that brewery because nobody's using it. But we found it was extremely difficult because of legalities, liens, ownership questions, yada yada yada," Malone said. "So we made several runs at trying to get in touch with the right people that could actually make it happen. We were unsuccessful."

The founders shifted their path and began to explore contract brewing. Huntsville's Olde Towne Brewing agreed, and Good People Beer appeared to be on the way.

The guys quickly blew through test cases of their amber ale, sharing it with friends for feedback. Next up, they intended to brew a test batch of the pale ale. Malone played hooky from his office job on July 5, 2007, waking before 5:00 a.m. and driving to Huntsville to brew. As he neared the halfway point, his phone rang.

"Jason, are you on the way?" an Olde Towne employee asked. Jason affirmed. "You might as well turn around." Why? "Because the brewery's on fire."

"Guys don't become even mild acquaintances with each other before they start playing tricks and jokes. I just thought it was a joke. I was like, shut up," Malone recalled. The employee convinced Malone that the fire was real, and the brewery's staff was in tears as they watched it burn. Malone continued on to Huntsville, arriving to see a building that "could not be more on fire than that place was." Good People's dreams literally went up in flames.

"It created a forcing mechanism that we had to put that aside and figure out how to get our original idea done because we didn't have the money or the time or the wherewithal to figure out anything else," Malone said.

This time, something clicked. Good People successfully acquired Southside Cellar's equipment and became Good People Brewing rather than Good

People Beer. The 1,900-square-foot brewery would soon resume working for the first time in eight years.

"We walked in for the first time, and our enthusiasm waned because it was a complete mess," Malone said. "It literally looked like they showed up to work one day and left that day without any inclination that they would never return again, only to never return again."

But there was hope: a data plate on the brew house indicated the manufacturer's name. Although the company had gone out of business, a little research helped the Good People founders identify the man who had originally installed the equipment. They persuaded the man, who lived in Florida, to return to the brewery and help fix things up.

"That was my educational crash course into brewery equipment," Malone said. It accelerated his learning curve as he moved from home brewer to commercial brewer. "Just like a home project or a car project, when someone shows you how to do it, it's really not that hard. But the intimidation of messing something up creates paralysis, and you won't go in there and just start working on your car," Malone said. "At the end of my eighteenth day working at the old place, the intimidation was totally gone."

With the equipment in working order, in March 2008, the Malone family—Jason, wife Kerri, their six-year-old and their infant—relocated to Birmingham.

And the brewing began. With twelve half barrels of Good People Brown Ale, Malone and Sellers thought they were set for some time. Sampling with friends, potential accounts, distributors and the 2008 Magic City Brewfest quickly depleted the supply. A batch of pale ale was fermenting, and because it took longer, it wasn't ready for the festival. Instead, Good People kegged it and sold it during a Five Points South neighborhood party on July 4, 2008—almost exactly a year after the original contract-brewing plan had evaporated. Once again, Birmingham was in the brewing business.

Thanks to the efforts of Free the Hops, Good People was set up for success unlike its predecessors. But the brewery's opening wasn't tied to the organization's work. "Quite frankly, I'm not sure if we knew about Free the Hops day one. But day two we did. They were the ones that had the vision, the manpower, the organizational skills, the foresight, the vision. We were just the fortunate benefactors of it," Malone said. "We became the brewery that was, by default, championed by them. They are most certainly responsible for a certain level of our success because they did the education out in the marketplace. They greased the tracks, big time."

Sellers agreed. "If it hadn't been for Free the Hops, we'd have probably been looking at a different outcome. The awareness they were providing the public was huge. That parallel really helped us. At the time, we were the only ones [brewing in Birmingham], so if you needed a news story about beer, you came to us," he recalled with a laugh. "We got a ton of press off that. It was good."

Likewise, the J. Clyde was already at work educating consumers about craft beer. Owner Jerry Hartley admitted he was nervous when he first heard a brewery was coming to town. "We were still struggling to build a market with people who hadn't bought into what we were doing here. We had no macro beers. We had no Bud or Coors," he said. Potential patrons would often leave and walk to the bar next door when they learned that American macro lagers weren't available. Finding beers to suit the pub's mission was also challenging. "I had forty taps, and we struggled to find beers to put on the wall," said Hartley. Because of limited options, at one point he had thirteen Rogue beers on tap.

But Hartley quickly made contact with the Good People owners, and the two became partners in building the market. The restaurant was often the first place consumers could taste a new Good People beer.

As Birmingham's only brewery, Good People also became a rallying point for craft beer fans. "It wasn't real, real difficult to go in some establishment, a grocery store or bar or whatever, and say, 'We're opening up a brewery' or 'We just opened up a brewery' and get their attention," Malone said. He joked that they realized a bigger space would be necessary by day two in the original location.

"It was designed to be a brewpub," he said. "The tale goes that ABC came in and said, 'You can't do this.' They said, 'Oh shit. We can't be a brewpub, but we can be a brewery, so we're going to put up this piece of glass between the two and become a brewery instead of a brewpub.'"

The adjacent restaurant became a brewery customer. The beer was brewed, sold to a distributor, loaded onto a truck and then sold back to the restaurant and other clients. Brewpubs are low-volume brewers, whereas breweries are high-volume service and production. "You couldn't get anything in and out of there quickly," Malone said. "Every keg that we took out of there was a singular keg on a dolly, down a huge hallway."

The space and the market were both issues for Southside Cellar. At that time, Malone said, you had two challenges of a successful brewery: make good beer but also convince people to drink it. There was significant education ahead, and the local palate wasn't developed. That immediately put Good People in a more competitive position, thanks to Free the Hops, which became Good People's de facto education arm, and regional breweries such as Sweetwater and Lazy Magnolia, which had established a clientele in Birmingham. "I don't see their [1990s breweries] product as a reflection of them going out of business," Malone said. "They had so much going against them."

Good People saw its client list grow quickly, including support from some prominent local players. Early on, James Beard Award–winning chef Frank Stitt's restaurants added Good People to its taps. "And it's not like he has thirty taps. I think at the time he had maybe four taps at Highlands," Melinda Sellers recalled. "Talk about an awesome friend to have."

Good People Brewing was off to a steady start. But Alabama beer restrictions—and therefore Birmingham brewing—still had a long way to go.

5
GOURMET BEER BILL

With its priorities set, Free the Hops began taking steps toward legislative change. The organization, with support from Harry Kampakis, hired lobbyist Michael Sullivan to have the Gourmet Beer Bill drafted and floated in the 2006 legislative session. Expectations were low—it was an election year, after all, and a pro-alcohol vote could be costly to a representative—but the first session would allow the group to gauge interest. Kampakis also brought Senator Steve French (R-Birmingham) to a Free the Hops meeting in order to educate the group on the process of passing a bill.

"I knew that there was a statehouse, and I knew that the legislature would have to vote on a bill at the start of it. But now I know every nuance of how a bill goes from nonexistent to law, and there are a lot of steps," Kline said.

But it was early yet, and support was growing. And that worked against the bill.

"Whether in the legislature or outside the legislature, hardly anybody understood craft beer. Everybody just assumed that it was a push to have cheap, high-alcohol beer," Kline said.

That first session helped the group identify allies, opponents and what would be necessary to advance the cause. The bill didn't leave committee that session, but as soon as it ended, Free the Hops began planning. Fundraising was ongoing, as was educating the citizenry to pull public opinion onto its side. That involved regular tastings, building a membership base and asking those members to contact their legislators to drum up support.

HOW A BILL BECOMES A LAW

A bill is first introduced in the House or the senate by a member of the state's legislature, typically the member who is sponsoring the bill. For strategic purposes, it is usually introduced in both bodies simultaneously. After its first reading, the bill is referred to committee. The appropriate committees are selected based on the bill's subject and financial impact. The committee considers the bill and must approve it before sending it back to the House or senate for a second reading. The bill is read for a third time, and members have the opportunity to debate before voting. If the bill passes, it is then sent to the other chamber, where the process is repeated. Once a bill has passed both chambers, it is sent to the governor for his signature or veto. If the governor opts to veto the bill, the legislature has an opportunity to overrule.

This wasn't the first time the legislature considered increasing the alcohol by volume limit for beer. In 1995, Miller and Anheuser-Busch butted heads regarding Alabama's alcohol by volume limit, which was then set at 5.0 percent. Miller wanted to increase it to 6.0 percent. "We have to brew beers specifically for Alabama," Miller spokesman Bob Hunt said to the Associated Press. But Larry Langford, then Fairfield mayor and Birmingham Budweiser public relations director, said that was no reason to increase the limit. Birmingham Budweiser's vice-president agreed with his PR director: "We're preaching moderation on one end, and then we're trying to raise alcohol content on the other side," he told the AP. Hunt pushed back, saying that Budweiser's position was a marketing ploy and based solely on reducing competition. At the time, Miller's Icehouse and Miller Lite Ice clocked in at 5.5 percent ABV, and it brewed a special 5.0 percent version for Alabama. The argument dated back to 1993.

The Yeas and Nays

Free the Hops, however, actively courted public opinion, and it showed. Kendra Cahill of Avondale wrote to the *Birmingham News* in 2006:

> *Don't the beer clubs in Alabama have as much right to hold fun, tasty meetings like those the wine clubs already hold? I think the answer is yes. The alcohol-by-volume limit for wine in Alabama is 14.9 percent. Shouldn't beer be treated the same way? The main factor holding down the beer lover's cause is resistance from the big beer distributors, which fear diminishing profits. Allowing gourmet beer in Alabama will not cause hosts of Super Bowl parties to spend money on India pale ales instead of* [insert generic beer here].

In a *Birmingham News* article, Michael Tomberlin wrote, "Craft beer drinkers mostly are looking to experience different flavors and savor varieties of beer rather than slamming down a six-pack at a time. For those who are looking for the effect of the alcohol, high-gravity beers bring the buzz with fewer beers."

The legislature, however, wasn't as quick to come around. Free the Hops started out lobbying for a 14.9 percent ABV limit, although the organization ultimately agreed to an amendment that created a 13.9 percent limit and restricted convenience store sales. "You have to accept from time to time that compromise is necessary. If you don't compromise, you don't get the ideal, you get nothing," then FTH president Stuart Carter said to the *Birmingham News*.

By 2007, the organization was ready to formally hire Sullivan as a lobbyist. He tempered its expectations, and sure enough, that year the bill won the Shroud Award, presented to the deadest bill in the House.

The arguments against the bill were largely predictable; Alabama is in the Bible belt, after all, and as of 2015, twenty-five of the state's sixty-seven counties were dry. In a letter to the *Birmingham News*, Mason Guttery wrote, "I am an Alabama native, a husband, a father and a Christian—and I absolutely love and respect beer…It is not a blue or red issue. It is an issue of choice and variety being needlessly restricted from each of us by obsolete, outdated ideals."

Alabama Citizen Action Program executive director the Reverend Joe Godfrey said the group opposed the measure. "Study after study has shown the more accessible alcohol is and the more potent it is, the more damage it does," he told the Associated Press. He expressed concern about high-gravity beers being marketed to young people.

Representative Richard Laird (D-Roanoke) seconded that notion: "We are killing our young people." However, other representatives disagreed. During a House debate, Representative Johnny Mack Morrow (D–Red Bay) argued that teenagers wouldn't pursue high-gravity beers: "If you think back to your teenage days, if you had the choice of buying a bottle of beer that costs ten dollars or a bottle of beer that costs fifty cents, which would you choose?"

"It doesn't lend itself to an underage crowd, a college crowd in a lot of ways, because it costs more," Free the Hops's Gabe Harris said. "Ninety-nine percent of college kids will say, 'I'd much rather drink that six-pack of Bud Light that costs half as much as the Good People,' or whatever brewery you want to think of. They don't market to those kind of people."

"When someone spends higher amounts on his beer, they want to taste it—they want to savor it—they do not toss it back and quickly reach for another," Wesley W. Wilson wrote in a letter to the *Huntsville Times*.

Stuart Carter, Free the Hops's second president who described himself to *Birmingham* magazine as a born-again Christian, said this wasn't a sin issue. "What was the first miracle Jesus did? He turned water into wine. It wasn't grape juice," he said. "I wouldn't expect anything else of the creator of the universe than the primo stuff."

Other opponents said that some communities wouldn't have the personnel to police issues such as drunken driving. And in 2008, Representative Alvin Holmes (D-Montgomery) uttered perhaps the most famous line during debate: "What's wrong with the beer we got? It drinks pretty good, don't it?"

Free the Hops had hosted a beer-tasting party the previous week, and whether because of interest in the beers themselves or other motives, many legislators supported the efforts.

Senator Lowell Barron (D-Fyffe) and Representative Jimmy Martin (D-Clanton) argued that the bill would increase tax revenue and economic development in small towns. In fact, in 2015, when an Alabama Supreme Court ruling challenged the wet status of some such municipalities, tax revenue was at the heart of some folks' concern.

"Nobody is making you drink, I don't put it in your face. I don't really advertise it," Missy Rutland, owner of Missy's Taste of Home in Fayette, said to AL.com. "Not all of them voted for it originally, but they don't want to be without the tax revenue, I can guarantee that." In Haleyville, the sales generated an extra $500,000 in revenue, a quarter of which went to purchasing school textbooks.

The financial gain could go beyond tax dollars, proponents said. Representative Thomas Jackson (D-Thomasville), a sponsor of the bill, said the legalization of such beer would be good for both tourism and recruiting businesses and people to the state.

But with a low ABV limit, that wouldn't happen in Alabama. In 2008, Stuart Carter told *Birmingham* magazine that at any given moment, about half of *Beer Advocate*'s top 30 beers were made in America. But of the top 100, the most he had seen available in Alabama was 15. About 300 beers were available in Alabama, but there were more than 180 beer styles and 20,000 known beers in the world.

"Craft beers are almost exclusively the domain of hobbyists and connoisseurs. They are commonly sold at a higher price and a lower quantity than more mainstream fare," wrote Greg Sirmon in a letter to the *Press-Register.*

The time and care put into craft beers limits profit margins, which is part of why it was difficult for Alabama's 1990s breweries to succeed.

"Small breweries thrive by innovation," Alabama Brewers Guild executive director Dan Roberts said to the *Birmingham News* in 2013.

Kline compared the appeal of such beers to drinking fine wine. "Selling more of a high-margin, high-quality product is going to be more profitable," he explained to the *Birmingham News.* "It's always been one of our arguments that there would be a net benefit in terms of economic impact and not just in terms of people being able to drink beer." His successor, Carter, echoed that sentiment. "It's not about getting loaded. It's about a very sensuous drink. I would put a well-crafted gourmet beer against any wine in the world," he told the Associated Press. Carter repeatedly argued that the price of high-alcohol beers put off binge drinkers.

Progress was slow but steady. By the end of the 2008 session, the bill had passed committees in both branches of the state legislature and made it through the House but not the senate and then the senate but not the House. "I had every reason to think, 'This is it. It's going to happen this year,'" Kline recalled. Free the Hops steeled itself for a fifth go-round, and Kline felt optimistic as the 2009 legislative session dawned.

"On a lot of things, I'm cynical. On this, I was the eternal optimist," he said. "I always felt like we were right on the cusp, it was just about to happen. I knew we were doing the right thing, and I knew we had support from the citizens."

During days when Free the Hops thought it likely that the bill would be debated, Kline turned on an audio stream of the debate and listened as he went throughout his day. The senate committee chairs approved the bill in week two of the fifteen-week session. The House Tourism and Travel Committee approved a similar bill within days. After moving out of committee, the bill cleared the House, and on May 14, it passed the senate. On the same day, the governor signed a bill that allowed an increase in the strength of table wine, from 14.9 percent ABV to 16.5 percent. Free the Hops and other proponents of the bill eagerly awaited his approval.

Governor Bob Riley signed the Gourmet Beer Bill into law on May 22, 2009. Free the Hops members and other craft beer fans flocked to de facto clubhouse the J. Clyde to celebrate.

"It's just one of the greatest moments of euphoria I've ever had in my entire life. After five years of having that bill in front of the legislature and four years ending in despair, a punch to the gut, increasingly loud choruses of naysayers who just assumed we weren't up to the task, to finally have it pass—there's no words to describe it. It was intense," Kline recalled. He lifted a glass of Ayinger Celebrator Doppelbock to mark the occasion. On the Friday night of the passage, Jerry Hartley offered specials at the J. Clyde.

The bill's opponents were predictably less thrilled. "I don't understand why everyone wants to keep expanding alcohol, but apparently it's an idol in America today," the Alabama Citizen Action Program's Godfrey said to the Associated Press.

ELEVATING THE MARKET

It took about a week for higher-gravity beers to reach store shelves. Birmingham Beverage already had about twenty high-gravity beers in stock because military bases in Alabama, clients of the distributor, weren't subject to the state laws. Owner Harry Kampakis said he began distributing those beers because he recognized a move toward craft beer in the rest of the nation. "That allowed us to establish a relationship with the brands before they entered Alabama," he explained to the *Birmingham Business Journal*. However, he and other distributors had to file paperwork with the Alabama Alcoholic Beverage Control Board before distributing widely.

By June, the J. Clyde had reported a 50 percent increase in business, and the high-gravity beers flew off shelves at Mountain Brook's Western Supermarket. "Customers would come up and buy it off the delivery cart. I knew there was a lot of anticipation for these quality beers, but I was surprised at just how well it's been received," Birmingham Beverage owner Harry Kampakis told the *Birmingham News*. Vulcan Beverage customers waited eagerly for the store to take inventory of its first shipment of such beers.

"This is not a whiskey town, and it's not a wine town. This is a beer town, and everybody is finally getting their beer," the shop's owner, Mark Green, said to the *Birmingham News*. Retailers were quick to acknowledge that the initial boom was because of the longtime ban on such beverages, but even so, they expected the economic benefits to last. Part of that was because high-gravity beers cost more.

The bill's effects were felt statewide. Shari Webster, owner of Mobile's Gourmet Galley, said summer sales at her small business increased 1,100 percent from the year prior. She attributed the success to gourmet beer. The area's Cottage Hill Package and Spring Hill Spirits, both owned by brothers Andrew and Michael Manas, saw beer sales nearly triple in the months following the law's passage. High-gravity beers accounted for 75 percent of beer sales in that time frame.

Draft beer-to-go, which tends to be fresher than its bottled companions, also increased in popularity. It became legal in 1980, but interest was renewed by the increased focus on beer legislation.

And since the bottle size restriction remained, some beers were available in Alabama following the Gourmet Beer Bill's passage only on draft because they were otherwise distributed in twenty-two-ounce bottles.

The number of stores offering draft-to-go grew as well following the bill's passage. In 2010, Birmingham's Highland Package Store wrested the title of most taps in the state from a Huntsville shop. Highland Package now offers fifty-two beers on tap.

"It's a new revenue stream. A lot of us thought the impact of the change in the alcohol law would be a mild bump," Dee's Package Store manager Chris Carlisle said to the *Birmingham News*. The shop's bestseller was still Bud Light, but business had certainly shifted. "But a lot of people we've never seen before are now coming in to buy high-gravity beer."

That was indicative of a market expansion, not a displacement of the same dollars, some retailers believed. "It's expanded the market because it's not replacing Coors Light and it hasn't really replaced wine with dinner," Western Supermarkets CEO Darwin Metcalf told the *Birmingham Business Journal*. "It's another option for the consumer."

Alabama Options

Another new-to-Alabama brewery seemed to enter the market every week, but one in particular drew great attention. Oskar Blues Brewery drummed up national attention, in part because it was the first microbrewery in the United States to opt for cans because they are more convenient, keep light and air out and are easier to recycle. But its addition to the local market was especially exciting for the brewery's owners because it started in a bathtub in a trailer in Auburn, where Dale Katechis brewed a pale ale. He started selling it at a Cajun restaurant he launched in 1999 in Lyons, Colorado. The beer's popularity grew into Oskar Blues.

However, because of limitations such as ABV, the Alabama native's beer, now marketed in conjunction with his brother, Chris, wasn't available in his home state. The well-regarded Dale's Pale Ale (named a favorite in a *New York Times* blind taste test) is 6.5 percent ABV, or 0.5 percent too much alcohol for Alabama at the time.

After the laws changed, the brewery ran into another problem: it was at full production capacity already to serve its existing customers. There simply wasn't enough beer to go around. The Katechis brothers ultimately cut distribution in Nevada and Idaho in order to free up enough product to distribute in Alabama. The beer debuted in their home state in July 2012.

The year also saw the introduction of Beer Engineers, a brewery that contract brewed through Gadsden's Back Forty Beer Co. In April before the launch, owner D.B. Irwin said he anticipated producing two hundred barrels a month and hoped to distribute to Georgia and Mississippi within a year. The company intended to sell high-gravity beers exclusively. In December 2012, the *Birmingham Business Journal* reported that Beer Engineers was on track to meet those projections by the summer of 2013. In 2013, the brewery also announced plans to open a $5 million facility, including a restaurant, next door to Good People in the 1932 Wood Wade Building.

However, production ceased in July 2014, and according to tweets sent from the company's Twitter account, the brewery didn't expect to immediately get back on track due to financial issues.

Two years after the Gourmet Beer Bill's passage, Chuck Geiss wrote in *Black & White City Paper*:

> One thing proven is that higher-alcohol content beer doesn't lead to a community of mindless drunks and teenagers driving into trees. It simply allows anyone who discriminates in their choice of upscale wines and good food, for example, to exercise the same discernment with high-end beers. It also provides consumers a choice they can easily find elsewhere in the country.

Even with that victory in hand, Free the Hops's battle raged on.

6
BREWERY MODERNIZATION ACT

Free the Hops initially identified alcohol limit and container size as its top priorities. After the success of the Gourmet Beer Bill, the organization considered continuing along that path. However, lobbyist Michael Sullivan recommended launching the Brewery Modernization Act instead. Because 2010 was an election year, the Gourmet Bottle Bill was unlikely to see much attention. However, the brewery efforts stood a better chance as a pro-business, economic initiative.

Dan Roberts, of both Free the Hops and Alabama Brewers Guild, explained that the Brewpub Act of 1992 was insufficient because it was so difficult to find an approved location. He, too, expected fairly quick progress with the Brewery Modernization Act since it focused on business operations rather than the alcohol itself. "We are severely limiting the growth of an industry that is finding success and creating jobs in other states," Roberts said to the *Birmingham News*. "It's really about making an environment more friendly for business, which ordinarily we would all be in favor of."

Five Alabama production breweries were in operation as the Brewery Modernization Act made the legislative rounds in 2011. But if visitors wanted to tour Good People, Madison's Blue Pants Brewery, Huntsville's Yellowhammer Brewing, Old Black Bear Brewing or Straight to Ale Brewing, they could admire brewing equipment without appreciating the fruit of its labor. State regulations meant breweries were unable to serve even a sample on site. And by 2011, all brewpubs had closed.

"Why are breweries and brewpubs under different legislation? At the end of the day, they both manufacture beer," Stuart Carter said to the *Birmingham News*.

"Everything about it [the Brewpub Act of 1992] is set up to make a brewpub fail," Carter told *Birmingham* magazine. Why should twenty-first-century businesses be bound to Prohibition-era precedents? The proposed legislation would loosen the historic district requirements and allow taprooms in breweries.

But the Brewery Modernization Act, which passed the senate, didn't get a final vote in the House because time ran out.

"Alabama law will not allow us to even charge $5 for a tour followed by free beer tastings like they can at wineries. Why are we treated differently?" Craig Shaw asked the *Birmingham News*. Shaw was brew master at Avondale Brewing Company, which was gearing up for business as the legislation went through the 2011 session.

That wasn't the only lost opportunity. Because of the existing laws, Alabama breweries—and therefore the state itself—missed out on tourism dollars, proponents said.

"In many states, breweries are tourist destinations. Our phones are ringing and our e-mail inboxes are filling with travelers looking for interesting places to stop while heading to the beach, in town for business, or looking for places to take their out-of-town guests. Currently we must deny their request for tours or to sample our products at the brewery," the Alabama Brewers Guild wrote in its statement supporting the Brewery Modernization Act.

"That's what it's all about—enabling Alabama business to grow," Roberts, the ABG's executive director, explained to the *Birmingham News*. "If you go to other states, taprooms are the most common thing in the world. Tasting rooms and tours are the way small breweries grow their brand. When you're dealing with beer on this level, it's not a commodity like the big beer brands."

"At a time when we need more job creation and economic activity, our laws are preventing growth in one of the industries that is trying to grow here," past Free the Hops president Stuart Carter said to the *Birmingham News*.

"It's taken the hard work of hundreds of craft beer makers several years to change things. Of the 50 million cases of beer sold in Alabama last year, wouldn't it be better if more of that revenue stayed in this state?" Back Forty's Jason Wilson asked the *News*.

The city's existing brewery and brewery-in-the-making both hoped to utilize freedoms a successful bill would offer. The repeal of brewpub laws would allow for on-site taprooms at Good People, Avondale and any breweries to come.

"At the end of the day it's about two things: economic development and competitiveness for Alabama businesses. It's a travesty we can't have a group of tourists stop by our brewery, show them around, sell them a pint of beer, talk to them about our brewery and Birmingham, tell them which grocery stores carry our products and recommend a great lunch stop or a hotel. We are constantly contacted by out-of-town people wanting to stop by the brewery to buy a pint of beer, and upon our explaining the restrictions of Alabama law, I doubt many people take the exit off of I-65," Good People brewmaster Jason Malone told *Black & White City Paper*. He noted that taproom revenue would help subsidize brewery growth.

Likewise, the paper noted that breweries could stimulate growth in other ways. "Avondale Brewing's [Coby] Lake says that he and his partners advocate SB 192 because they have spent considerable dollars to renovate a building that could easily become a hotspot in a Birmingham neighborhood that has been challenged for years," the paper's Chuck Geiss wrote.

Free the Hops's Gabe Harris explained in the same article:

> *The Brewery Modernization Act will help create jobs and revive dying neighborhoods in local communities. In addition, this bill allows brewpubs to provide tours and samples, which in turn would increase receipts from such taxes that go straight into Alabama's education fund. Existing data supports how the earlier legislation has benefited the businesses that are now carrying these beers and all the things that our opponents once railed against simply haven't happened.*

Budweiser Boycott

The act's proponents ran into another obstacle before the bill could come up for vote, and a surprising one: an area distributor. In April 2011, Birmingham Budweiser, the local Anheuser-Busch distributor, worked against the bill. Gadsden's Back Forty Brewing co-founder Jason Wilson said distributors worried that, with breweries being allowed to sell beer on premises, larger breweries like Anheuser-Busch and Coors could challenge the three-tier system. That system requires manufacturers to sell their beer to distributors, which then sell to stores. If breweries were permitted to self-distribute, Wilson explained to the Mobile *Press-Register*, distributors could see their business decline.

Free the Hops (by then 1,700 members strong) quickly called for a boycott of all beer carried by Birmingham Budweiser, which meant not only avoiding products such as Budweiser but also national and even local favorites, including Back Forty.

Harris told *Black & White City Paper*:

> *Anheuser-Busch and their individual distributors have every right to work the legislature against the Brewery Modernization Act. They can be opposed to a jobs-creating, economic development bill that would benefit local business. They can oppose craft beer and Free the Hops. But the craft beer community and Free the Hops can oppose them too. Anheuser-Busch products and products from their distribution network are now banned from Free the Hops events. This will have its first big effect on the Rocket City Brewfest and will continue with the Magic City Brewfest unless the Brewery Modernization Act becomes law in a form we find acceptable.*
>
> *The state can support many more breweries and we think it is in the best interest of consumers, the economy and the state to see [the legislation] move forward.*

(In 2012, the Alabama Wineries Association called for a similar boycott on beers distributed by opponents to a bill that some said aimed to create an exception to the three-tier system for wineries alone.)

It wasn't a decision Free the Hops members took easily, the organization's Stuart Carter explained to the *Birmingham News*:

> *The only power we have is the content of our wallets. What we're saying with this boycott is we as consumers don't want to be channeling profits to wholesalers who are using those profits to prevent other consumers from getting the beer we want to drink. This is hurting friends, either friends we know or friends who brew the beer we love to drink. The problem is they're the innocents in this who are caught in the crossfire.*

Those beers would have been excluded from Huntsville's Rocket City Brewfest and Birmingham's Magic City Brewfest had negotiations not resulted in a compromise prior to the events. But within weeks, the parties reached an agreement. Free the Hops conceded to maintain a distinction between brewpubs and production breweries. As a result, breweries were allowed to offer tastings without restriction or an additional license, but sales were limited to on-site consumption. Draft-to-go must still be purchased elsewhere. Brewpubs, on the other hand, still faced a number of the existing restrictions. Some were modified: the historic requirement was expanded to include economically distressed areas as determined by the municipality, not just a historic building; they were allowed to sell to wholesalers for outside distribution; and while a restaurant was still necessary, the minimum seating requirement was eliminated. This compromise was necessary in part because distributors wanted the brewpub license to remain special and limited.

On the Free the Hops blog, Alabama Brewers Guild executive director Dan Roberts wrote that the bill's sponsor, Senator Bill Holtzclaw (R-Madison), favored the economically distressed area addition. "Does an area with an empty building—a building that would be perfect for a brewpub—constitute an economically distressed area? That's up to a city council," Roberts wrote.

In addressing the media, he explained that the compromise was preferable to the alternative. "It will not be everything we wanted, but it is definitely a workable solution and represents a significant improvement over the current restrictions," he told the *Birmingham News*. "We were not going to get everything we wanted. The bill we ended up with is still a vast improvement over what we currently have."

Jason Malone echoed those sentiments in an interview with the paper. "Anything in the right direction is better than the current status quo. Obviously, some compromises did have to be made, and while we would have rather not had to give up anything that we were going after, that's not realistic."

Moving Forward

Birmingham Budweiser became a top-level member of Free the Hops after the gourmet beer boycott, and the legislation gained forward momentum. On June 1, 2011, the Brewery Modernization Act passed the senate and awaited Governor Robert Bentley's signature. Many worried that he would veto the bill, but Bentley explained that responsibilities as governor differed from those of state representative. "When I represented my local community, I voted against Sunday alcohol sales and things of that nature," he said to the *Birmingham News*. "As governor, it's a little bit different. I don't feel I should impose my views on everybody in the state. The legislature has had a chance to look at it and passed it. I'm sure I will sign it."

He did so, and Free the Hops again celebrated success. "It's the biggest change in Alabama brewing laws since the repeal of Prohibition," then Free the Hops president Gabe Harris told the Associated Press.

The bill was expected to result in more breweries and brewpubs opening in the state. The bill opened up the viability of the businesses by creating additional revenue opportunities.

"The state will be able to print a beer tour map of the state where people can go from Huntsville to Mobile visiting brew pubs and breweries," Carter said to the Associated Press.

Meanwhile, Kline also rejoiced in the organization's success. "We went from taking five years on a bill to taking two years on a bill," Kline said. "There was starting to be some clear economic impact from craft beer that people could see and quantify. Free the Hops had gained the reputation of only advocating bills that do good things, as opposed to bills that do bad things. So it got easier each time," Kline said.

The economic impact was evident almost immediately: the state's brewery production increased by 672.19 percent in the year following the bill's passage. Following the passage of the bill, brewpubs were able to sell beer to wholesalers, which could then distribute the beer. It didn't stop there. Between 2012 and 2013, United States breweries increased production by nearly 15.00 percent, and in Alabama, the growth was even more significant: at 22.35 percent. "The thing that I think has spawned all of the growth in the industry is the taprooms. That really gives you a ready revenue source rather than having to wait 30 days for a wholesaler to pay," Good People Brewing Co. co-owner Michael Sellers told the Associated Press. He said the brewery's taproom would create additional jobs, and his business partner, Jason Malone, indicated expectations for continued growth. "I'm excited about where the market is headed in Alabama as people get more tuned into how much better craft beer is. We've come a long way and I think this trend is here to stay," he said to the *Birmingham News* as Avondale prepared to open.

Although Avondale debuted later that year, it was far from the last brewery to reap the legislation's benefits. Although only five breweries existed in Alabama as the Brewery Modernization Act began circulating through the legislature, thirteen were in operation by 2014.

In 2014, Alabama Brewers Guild president and Back Forty co-founder Jason Wilson attributed that to the act. "So when you prohibit these small microbreweries from doing things like selling pints at their production facility, that's the difference between a profitable and an unprofitable business model. The slightest restriction you impose on them can mean the difference between it being successful and failing," he told *Business Alabama*. "Since these pieces of legislation have passed, we haven't seen a single brewery shut down in the last five years. That's a testament to the impact this legislation has had."

Left: The filter in the foreground belonged to Abita Brewing Co., which contracted with Birmingham Brewing. *Steve Betts.*

Below: Birmingham Brewing boasted a capacity of 7,500 barrels. *Steve Betts.*

Above: Hop City's Growlertown features a frequently changing menu of sixty draft beers. *Author's collection.*

Left: The designs of Magic City Brewfest's tasting glasses change each year. *Gabe Harris.*

Above: The J. Clyde's back patio includes plastic walls and heaters for the winter but is spacious and airy in warmer months. *Jerry Hartley.*

Right: The J. Clyde was the first Alabama restaurant or bar that set craft beer as its top priority. *Brent Boyd.*

When the J. Clyde renovated its back bar, Jerry Hartley thought the room's thirteen taps would be sufficient for all Alabama beers. Alabama breweries quickly proved him wrong. *Brent Boyd.*

Above: Good People Brewing's tap handles embody the brewery's laid-back southern style. *Paul MacWilliams.*

Right: Good People Brewing's day-to-day operations are managed by Michael Sellers and Jason Malone. *Wes Frazer.*

Good People, the state's largest brewery, temporarily closed in early 2015 to renovate its taproom. This is the room before changes. *Photography courtesy of Constellation ImageWorks.*

The first Hops for Honeys meeting was held May 2010 at Rogue Tavern. *Melinda Sellers.*

Above: Good People was the
first modern-day Birmingham
brewery to offer its wares in
cans. *Photography courtesy of
Constellation ImageWorks.*

Right: Good People has
steadily increased its capacity
over the years. In 2013, it
produced 8,500 barrels of
beer. *Gabe Harris.*

Good People has hosted events during Food Blog South, a conference for food bloggers (renamed "Food Media South" in 2015). *FoodBlogSouth via a Creative Commons License.*

Avondale Brewing's massive outdoor stage is often the site for concerts that draw crowds. *Telegraph Branding.*

Avondale Brewing cofounder Hunter Lake. *Telegraph Branding.*

Avondale Brewing cofounder Coby Lake. *Telegraph Branding.*

Left: Miss Fancy's Tripel is one of Avondale Brewing's highest-alcohol beers. Bartenders sometimes suggest mixing it with another of the brewery's offerings—to interesting results. *Telegraph Branding.*

Below: Avondale Brewing's taproom is a popular hangout for young professionals, neighborhood residents and more. *Telegraph Branding.*

A massive outdoor bar quickly proved necessary for Avondale Brewing, which in nice weather is often packed with hundreds of people at a time. *Telegraph Branding.*

Cahaba Brewing, currently located on Third Avenue South, will relocate in 2015 to a larger facility. *Paul MacWilliams.*

The partners' love of the outdoors shows up in Cahaba Brewing's branding, including paddle-inspired tap handles. *Paul MacWilliams.*

Above and below, left: Each brewery offers a number of styles, and a flight is the perfect way to get a sense of what's best. *Paul MacWilliams.*

Below, right: Cahaba Brewing's five partners maintain day jobs outside of the brewery. They say it's a passion project. *Paul MacWilliams.*

Although it doesn't yet fill the space, Trim Tab Brewing owner Harris Stewart estimates the brewery could hold equipment to brew sixty thousand barrels of beer annually. *Brad Lovell Photography.*

A Trim Tab employee pours hops into a container. Along with water, barley and malt, these are essential beer ingredients. *Brad Lovell Photography.*

Trim Tab's tasting gallery features rotating art exhibits. The brewery doesn't charge a gallery fee, and shows last two to three months. *Brad Lovell Photography.*

Trim Tab intends its space to be a gathering place, where ideas can be born and people are inspired. *Brad Lovell Photography.*

Several Trim Tab beer names are inspired by history. ESB Fox and Furnace, for example, uses an English-sounding name for the most popular English beer style during Birmingham's founding. *Brad Lovell Photography.*

In 2014, Trim Tab funded this "It's nice to have you in Birmingham" mural with a Kickstarter.com crowdfunding campaign. Local group Magic City Mural Collective painted the mural. *Brad Lovell Photography.*

7

AVONDALE BREWING CO.

A brewery's wares can tell a story, and at Avondale Brewing Co., that becomes obvious quickly.

Step one: taste Spring Street Saison. The flagship beer is a reflection of the history of the neighborhood for which the business is named. Forty-first Street, on which the brewery now sits, was originally known as Spring Street and served as the hub of the fledgling town of Avondale's business district. The area was founded in 1887, incorporated as a town in 1889 and annexed into Birmingham in 1907—the year of the state's largest beer production to date.

Much like Birmingham, Avondale was formed around train tracks. The Alabama Great Southern Railway cut through one end of the neighborhood, bisecting Spring Street. The road culminated at Avondale Park, which included the spring from which the street drew its name. Its water is pure and credited with saving lives in the cholera epidemic of 1873. The park once also housed the elephant Miss Fancy, the inspiration for Avondale Brewing's tripel. She was bought off a circus owner and eventually became part of the area zoo. Miss Fancy was purchased by the Birmingham Advertising Club, which was putting on an industrial exposition at the time. The promoters believed she would garner more interest than the mill, factory, furnace and mines already committed to the event. The neighborhood's children raised $500 of Miss Fancy's $2,000 purchase price. During Prohibition, police offers were said to provide whiskey for Miss Fancy and her keeper, John Todd.

The brick exterior of Avondale Brewing Co. had to be almost wholly reconstructed before the brewery could open. *Telegraph Branding.*

Nell Barron Griswold sits atop Miss Fancy, the beer-drinking elephant, in Avondale Park. *Birmingham, Alabama Public Library Archives.*

"John and Miss Fancy, it seems, were taking their usual toddle over the hills just back of the zoo, and it must be confessed that before they left, they both had been partaking of the white lightning that cherish the heart and machete mad the spirit," James Saxon Childers wrote in a 1934 *Birmingham News-Age Herald* article. Todd, the elephant's full-time keeper, was the only black trainer in the country by the time the 1934 article was published. Todd was revered as the only person who could elicit a response from Miss Fancy. Avondale Brewing's double IPA bears his name.

Nearby, the neighborhood saw a few drops of blood shed during the Civil War, when the sheriff's wife was struck by a stray bullet during a skirmish. (She survived.) That's now reflected by Avondale Battlefield IPA.

The building in which the brewery is housed, with a history dating to 1895, previously was home to Avondale Bank & Savings Company, a grocery store, Avondale Lodge, a furniture repair shop and Longbranch Saloon, which closed in the 1980s. The latter's name appears on the brewery's Scottish ale.

Is that a lot to take in? Avondale Brewing invites patrons to slow down and appreciate the history, one beer at a time.

"We want to reflect all the great aspects of the area from the past, present and future," the brewery proclaimed in its written history. "Avondale Brewing Company sees the potential growth in Avondale after its dormant states during the depression and the city's withdrawal of support for the park during the 60s and 70s, leading to a downturn of its community feel to run-down apartments inhabited with drug dealers, addicts, homeless, and criminals."

"We knew that successful breweries and successful businesses generally have a story. Beer being one of the most social businesses you can have, you want to have a story behind it," Hunter Lake elaborated to *Alabama Alumni Magazine*.

BUILDING BUSINESS

Avondale's owners determined that 201 Forty-first Street South was the ideal brewery location, but it took a lot of work to prepare the building, which had been vacant since the 1980s. The building's facade was crumbling and required brick-by-brick reconstruction in order to meet code and historical standards. The foundation had to be repaired, and the building's interior columns had to be reinforced. A new roof, plumbing, electrical fixtures and more were also necessary to bring the building to code and health department standards.

Although its history is rich, the brewery may not have existed at all were it not for Free the Hops legislation. Avondale Brewing was inspired by the 2009 Gourmet Beer Bill, and in April 2011, brothers Coby and Hunter Lake and business partner Chris Donaldson said they were prepared to open as soon as the city approved. The beers debuted at Magic City Brewfest that year, with renovations and recipe development ongoing as the group cleared legal hurdles. They poured from the J. Clyde's yellow fire truck, a signature at the event, and offered tastes of an IPA, saison and a few Belgian test beers. The event allowed the brewers to get feedback and tweak recipes as needed.

The brewery's opening was months away, which meant time for the Brewery Modernization Act to proceed through the legislature. Its success opened up additional options for Avondale, which had originally planned an off-site taproom across Forty-first Street from the brewery.

The taproom opened on November 4, 2011, and the owners anticipated brewing 1,500 barrels in the first year. Within a month of opening, they expected to double capacity. The beers served showed the influence of brewmaster Craig Shaw's

Brothers Coby and Hunter Lake have used their passion for craft beer and a good time to lead the way in revitalizing the Avondale neighborhood. *Telegraph Branding.*

travels. Shaw, a home brewer of more than a decade, drew inspiration from a trip to Belgium and Germany in 1998. Since he couldn't find comparable beers on Alabama shelves, he began home brewing to re-create those flavors. Spring Street Saison originated from that work.

The brewing philosophy was an important component of the business, Hunter Lake told *Alabama Alumni Magazine*: "We wanted beer that would bring you in so you could enjoy craft beer, act as a gateway. We wanted our beers to act as a gateway and be able to educate the mindshare of consumers out there."

And quickly, the brewery established itself as a gateway not just for craft beer fans but also for systemic change. Avondale Park reopened almost simultaneously, thanks to a $3 million grant secured by Friends of Avondale Park. The two became pillars of the community at opposite ends of the street.

"It was that extra spark that really united everybody together," Hunter Lake said to *Birmingham* magazine. "We could get a lot of people in there and attract a lot of people to this great neighborhood."

NEIGHBORHOOD REVITALIZATION

"I see Avondale Brewery as huge for Avondale," Merrillee Challis told the *Birmingham News* before the brewery's opening. Challis, along with her brother Brad and then boyfriend Brian Teasley, opened popular music venue Bottletree Café blocks away in 2006. "It can be an anchor as we slowly revitalize 41st Street."

Through their Turn Key Homes, which rehabilitates distressed properties, the Lake brothers purchased and rehabilitated a number of buildings along Forty-first Street, playing a role in fulfilling the vision Challis described. "What we're trying to do is bring this area back by making world-class beers," Avondale brew master Craig Shaw said to the Mobile *Press-Register*. The neighborhood's rich history had over time been replaced by a reputation for prostitution, crime and other ills.

"Avondale's the perfect example of how a brewery and the people behind a brewery have turned a neighborhood totally around. I really believe beer has been a huge, huge part of revitalization of Birmingham," Free the Hops's Gabe Harris said. "You can go talk to people because they're there for the same reasons you are. It's not like it's a restaurant or a bar. They sought out a brewery for specific reasons, to drink that brewery's beer in that area of town. They have a kinship."

The brothers continued that effort by partnering with development agency Main Street Birmingham to give away six months of rent in a retail space across from the brewery. The brothers initially expected to use the space as a tasting room, but the Brewery Modernization Act made that unnecessary. The winner, Freshfully, opened a market and café in the space.

In a CityLab.com piece, writer Matt Stroud pointed to *Cities Back from the Edge: New Life for Downtown* by Robert Brandes Gratz and Norman Mintz, in which the writers note, "When stores fill up and customer traffic increases, new activity is generated. People return to Main Street for more than the errand. Each element feeds and reinforces the other. A critical mass of economic activity evolves, and the downtown whole becomes stronger than the sum of its parts."

Freshfully closed in January 2014, but by then, a number of other businesses occupied the street. Now, Forty-first Street includes event venue the Nest and its bakery Baking Bandits; church-run coffee shop the Abbey; a church; restaurants such as Post Office Pies, Melt, Wasabi Juan's, Saw's Soul Kitchen and Avondale Grill; 41st Street Pub; and the Painted Shovel shop. In 2015, the space formerly home to Freshfully will be occupied by music venue and bar Saturn, as well as its coffee shop companion, Satellite.

"You have a built-in customer base because the brewery is so big and they have so many people over there," Wasabi Juan's owner Kelly Viall told the *Birmingham News*.

By 2013, the area also saw a surge in home sales. Elisa Macon of Walton Brown Real Estate told the *News* that Avondale Brewing's Lake brothers were in part responsible for that positive growth due to their business interests.

That hard work paid off with national recognition. An April 2013 *Southern Living* article dubbed Avondale a "next great neighborhood," drawing attention, both local and national, to the area. In 2014, it was one of five Birmingham bars listed on the magazine's list of the one hundred best in the South.

Brewing Boom

Just like the neighborhood it calls home, Avondale Brewing has also seen significant growth. The Birmingham Design Review Committee approved plans for the brewery's outdoor stage in April 2013, and it's now common to hear live music throughout the neighborhood, particularly on mild Saturdays. Events are common at the brewery, which can now host them in the spacious patio area, the upstairs private room or in the taproom.

Hunter Lake credits, in part, the brothers' fraternity experience at Sigma Alpha Epsilon with the brewery's events inspiration: "The party scene in Alabama allowed me to see the lack of the party scene in Birmingham as far as, there wasn't anything to do on the weekends or in the afternoons in Birmingham. You had to wait till dinner to have a party going on," he said. The brewery addresses that through its regular events and relationships with other vendors, such as Hunter's Red Mountain Crawfish Company, food trucks and more.

The property also houses canning and bottling lines, with a fifteen-barrel tank dedicated to bottling production. Spring Street Saison was released in bombers in October 2013, more than a year after the Gourmet Bottle Bill's passage. (It took longer than expected to gain approval because of a backlog in Montgomery, where the Alabama Alcoholic Beverage Control board must approve labels.) "Literally, everyone from volunteers to bartenders crowded into the bottling room, helping to make sure all went smoothly and to witness the culmination of everyone's hard work and dreams as they became reality," Shaw said in a prepared statement.

"There's an elegance about it," assistant brewmaster Eric Baumann told the *Birmingham News*. "With a bomber, you have two-and-a-quarter, two-and-a-half pints in there, and you're going to want to share it with your friends."

The Vanillaphant Porter followed in November of that year, and in late 2014, Battlefield IPA and Pachyderm Pale Wheat were canned, in part for the environmental and economic advantages, with plans to reassess and potentially add more styles to the canning line the following spring. In 2013, Zerve.com published a Buzzed story that identified Miss Fancy's Tripel as the beer most representative of Alabama. Meanwhile, the 2014 Craft Beer Awards International Craft Beer Competition awarded Meredith Marzen a gold medal, Longbranch Scottish Ale a gold, No Joka Mocha Stout a gold and French Oak Barrel-Aged Brett Saison a silver. The staff had grown to nearly forty people, including bartenders, by late 2014.

In 2012, Avondale Brewing told the *Birmingham Business Journal* that it hoped to have a 20 to 30 percent share of Alabama's craft beer market within five years. But even with exponential growth that is often credited with creating a more vibrant neighborhood, the Lake brothers said they want to proceed wisely.

Coby Lake explained:

> So yes, you have to manage the numbers and manage the growth. But at the same time, you have to make a determination of when enough is enough. In other words, we could continue to grow. But if we're satisfied where we are, there's no reason to push. We would obviously just slowly and naturally grow, but quality of life and not just being stressed out all the time plays into those decisions. We've pushed and pushed and pushed and pushed, and we've worked so hard the past three years. We may not take a break, but just not push so hard where we're growing and it's out of control. But we knew we had to get to a place where we're sustainable.

With the brewery, its parking lot and businesses its owners have helped recruit now occupying the better part of a city block, who knows what could be ahead?

8
GOURMET BOTTLE BILL

Before the Brewery Modernization Act was even approved, in 2011, Free the Hops began collaborating with the Alabama Brewers Guild and Alabama Wholesale Beer Association on a bill to address beer container size. The Gourmet Bottle Bill would increase the container size limit for beer from 16.0 ounces to 25.4 ounces. The 16.0-ounce bottle limit went into effect in 1936, Alabama Beverage Control Board assistant general counsel Bob Martin told the *Birmingham News*. The requested increase intentionally excluded 40.0-ounce containers, which typically contain malt liquor and often have negative connotations. Much like the Gourmet Beer Bill did in 2009, the Gourmet Bottle Bill would also open up distribution for beers currently unavailable in Alabama. Alabama was the only state that didn't allow purchases of larger-sized beer bottles.

Or at least, they were outlawed in most of the state. The Alabama Brewers Guild identified thirteen counties that had local legislation allowing larger containers. The number of exceptions added support to the bill, as proponents argued that it made sense to legalize larger containers statewide. Alabama breweries also expressed interest in larger containers. At the time, the state had forty-one wet counties, meaning that the thirteen counties with exceptions constituted nearly one-third of the wet portion of the state.

Good People began offering its County Line brews in 2010. A Coosa County convenience store on U.S. 280 carried the twenty-two-ounce bottles, the first batch of which sold out in four days. The series highlighted rare, unusual beers. "We wanted something special enough it's worth driving two hours to buy it," Good People brewmaster Jason Malone said to the *Birmingham News*. The beer was brewed in twenty-gallon batches, as opposed to the brewery's standard two hundred plus gallons. It was a return to home brewing roots for Good People's owners.

"We put it in trucks and left a perfectly willing customer base here, drove past a number of stores that would have loved to have sold it but couldn't because of these nonsensical laws," Jason Malone told the *Birmingham News*. "To do that on a small scale is too labor intensive to be practical."

"I have to admit I've driven from Birmingham to Coosa County to buy a beer brewed in Birmingham. That's absurd," Stuart Carter said to the *Birmingham News*.

But why would anyone care about a beer's bottle size? High-end beers are sometimes sold in larger, single bottles instead of in six-packs because the six-packs would be cost prohibitive. Limited release and seasonal beers are often packaged in such a way.

"American craft breweries doing Belgian-style beer love to bottle in the 750s because they can do the caged-and-corked look that resembles a bottle of champagne," Carter told the *Birmingham News*. Both Good People and Avondale planned to produce 750s. The brewery delayed its packaging plans in hopes of the bill passing, and its first packaged beers were, in fact, bombers.

As with other beer-related legislation, Free the Hops members viewed container size not just as a matter of choice but also as an economic measure.

"The thing that's most important isn't the beer. I may be burned as a heretic for saying that. But the most important thing is the business opportunities and the jobs that are created," Carter said to the *Birmingham News*.

"As with all of our bills, this is an economic development issue. This is not about the alcohol, this is about the economic opportunities and the jobs being created," he said in another interview with the paper.

The measure gained support from each leg of the brewing system, with representatives of each present at the House committee session to hear the bill. "We have all four tiers of the three-tier system. We've got the breweries, we've got the wholesalers, we've got the retailers and, oh yeah, the people who buy the stuff," Carter said told *Birmingham News*, whose editorial supported the bill. It wrote that the state's beer laws were out of date and held back the craft beer industry.

Mobile's *Press-Register*, a sister paper to the *News*, wrote in its 2012 editorial:

> *When Abita produced its 22-ounce "Save Our Shores" beer as a charitable nod to the Gulf states after the BP oil spill, no one could buy it in Alabama.*

> *That's because the state has some of the most ridiculously antiquated liquor laws in the country, including a unique 16-ounce restriction on the size of beer bottles…Allowing beer to be purchased in larger containers isn't a scary proposition. It would not suddenly release a floodgate of beer drinking in the state. Consumers already have access to the same quantity of beer, just in different packaging. Approving the bill would, however, let Alabama participate fully in the popular craft beer market, which makes it an economic development issue.*

"Gourmet beer aficionados typically sip these beers to enjoy the flavor, not to get drunk quicker. People who drink to get drunk typically do not buy gourmet beers. They will usually buy a 12-pack of cheap beer, which will do just fine," Billy Vance wrote in a letter to the *Birmingham News*.

Support didn't stop there; Atlanta-based Hop City Craft Beer and Wine also sent a representative to the committee. He said 12 percent of the Atlanta store's business came from Alabama, and 32 percent of the store's business came from larger containers.

"It's because of this bill passing that we're coming to Alabama this year. If we didn't think it was going to pass in 2012, we wouldn't be coming there. It's that simple," Hop City CEO Kraig Torres told the *Birmingham News*.

Unsurprisingly, opponents continued to voice concerns. DuWayne Bridges (R-Valley) filibustered the bill in 2012, arguing that larger containers would lead to more drunk driving accidents, as people might think they could drive after having one or two of these large beers. He also said it would appeal to youth.

In a letter to the *Press-Register*, Semmes resident Trey Thornton likewise expressed concern:

> *This issue is being described as one that will allow only for "gourmet beers." However, should this bill pass, what we will see is 24-ounce cans of very high-alcohol products on the shelves of our stores (for example, 24-ounce cans of Four Loko, which has 12 percent alcohol). That is the equivalent of more than 4½ regular 12-ounce beers in one serving. All one needs to do to see the effects of passage of a "gourmet bottle" bill is drive to Georgia or Florida and stop in one of their convenience stores. You won't see many "gourmet bottles," but you'll see shelf after shelf of low-priced 24-ounce cans of high-gravity beers.*

(His argument failed to take into consideration that the Gourmet Beer Bill limited convenience store sales.)

"Some beer dealers are urging the Alabama Legislature to pass a law allowing the size of beer containers to be increased from 16 fluid ounces to 25 fluid ounces. One result of such a law would be drinkers could get drunk quicker," J.E. Powell Jr. wrote in a letter to the *Birmingham News.*

Proponents echoed the defenses uttered with regard to previous legislation. In a letter to the *Huntsville Times*, Theodore F. Kearley wrote, "The liberation of beer laws in the state will also allow for the fledgling brewery industry in the state to create products that appeal to a wider audience and allow restaurants to carry a wider selection of beers, both of which would increase revenues for the state."

The bill failed in 2011, its first year. Despite detractors, the bill passed the Senate in late February 2012 with a single vote as the deciding factor. Governor Robert Bentley signed it into law on May 16, 2012.

"The governor does not drink alcohol and has no taste for beer, but he had no problems with this bill as it was written," the governor's representative Jeremy King said to the *Birmingham News*.

Carter told the *News*:

> *The Gourmet Bottle Bill, now that it has been signed into law by Gov. Bentley, is going to enable Alabamians to consume the best in the world. It will allow the thriving and quickly growing Alabama breweries to present their product in a competitive way to win market share on the national stage. The bottom line is this is going to put money into the Alabama economy and create jobs. We're going to let people achieve their dreams by letting their businesses thrive.*

By the time of passage, ten breweries were open or planned in the state, and Carter said every dollar spent on craft beer in the state created five dollars because of the associated jobs. About 3 percent of beer sold in Alabama at that time was craft, but Carter told the *Birmingham News* that it was growing at a rate of about 30 percent annually. D.B. Irwin, owner of the relatively short-lived Beer Engineers, said that day, "I'm looking at glass today so I can be one of the first to start producing in the 750ml size. The Gourmet Bottle Bill passage is definitely going to be an economic boom for us."

Bombers debuted on Alabama shelves on August 1, 2012, with some stores opening at midnight to celebrate. The J. Clyde began selling just after midnight, and co-owner Jerry Hartley said they had stocked up in anticipation. They carried about two dozen varieties of bombers at that time. At least two hundred new beers total were available in the state, based on information provided by AlaBev, Birmingham Beverage Co.'s craft beer arm.

Huntsville breweries Straight to Ale, Yellowhammer Brewing and Blue Pants Brewery created a collaboration series in celebration of the Gourmet Bottle Bill's passage. Each brewed a special release at its individual brewery—Straight to Ale's English Barleywine, Blue Pants' Wee Heavy, Yellowhammer's Belgian Quadrupel—and finished with the Liberation Smoked Dopplebock, which used a recipe they crafted via e-mail discussion. Proceeds were donated to the Land Trust of North Alabama.

The Gourmet Bottle Bill completed Free the Hops's legislative agenda. "We'll sit down after this session and talk about what we can do for craft beer in general," then president Gabe Harris said to the Associated Press. Whether that meant continuing to lobby for fewer brewing restrictions or continuing to serve as an entity for consumer education, the organization had much to celebrate. As the organization's Dan Roberts told the Associated Press, "Between 2008 and now, it's really a whole new world."

9
CAHABA BREWING CO.

Cahaba Brewing Co. is a feat of passion, and that's reflected in the company's name. The Cahaba River is the source for much of Birmingham's drinking water and therefore for the beer the company produces. But it's also personal to the brewery's owners: managing partner Eric Meyer has canoed or walked the river's route from Springville to Helena. He and business partner Andy Gwaltney, early in their friendship, would often spend weekends canoeing the river, and each of the partners is an outdoorsman of sorts. Like the river and the state's diverse ecosystems, Cahaba Brewing is an amalgamation of its owners' interests and stylistic influences.

Gwaltney and Meyer met through message boards on the Free the Hops website and soon started going in together to buy grain in bulk for home brewing.

"I think a lot of home brewers have a dream of owning their own place one day," Meyer said, and such conversations were a natural evolution of the pair's friendship. Other friends, including lawyer Burton Dunn, Taylor DeBoer and Jacob Hayes, joined in, and the process moved quickly.

"We were sitting in Eric's garage drinking the beer he made and it is great stuff," Dunn recalled in conversation with the *Birmingham Business Journal*. "Originally, they came up with the idea of purchasing a system and just making it for ourselves, then you could see what was happening around the state and we thought it would be a good time to enter the market."

The partners reached out to Free the Hops founder Danner Kline, who was by then working for distributor Birmingham Budweiser, seeking advice.

Cahaba Brewing Co. made its debut at the 2012 Magic City Brewfest. *Gabe Harris.*

Soon after, during a Magic City Brewfest weekend, Gwaltney learned that Huntsville brewery Straight to Ale was selling its equipment. Meyer traveled to Huntsville, inspected the equipment and immediately put down a deposit. Never mind that Cahaba Brewing didn't have a name or a facility—the wheels were in motion.

The Cahaba partners began working with real estate agents to find a building, but the eight-thousand-square-foot former home furnishing store they ended up occupying caught Meyer's eye. Once the other four partners had visited it and approved, design and build-out were underway—two months after the group decided to open a brewery. (Their wives were probably relieved to get home brewing equipment out of their kitchens and garages; both Meyer and Gwaltney began brewing in 2007 and said equipment quickly took over.)

The Cahaba partners acquired the building in October 2011, began construction in January and ran pilot batches in April. Cahaba debuted its Liquidambar, Ryzeome Rye Stout and Oka Uba IPA at the 2012 Magic City Brewfest, one year after the brewing equipment's sale set the dream in motion. The taproom celebrated its grand opening on September 29, 2012.

"Being able to make something and see through its process, this final product then you can enjoy almost like a carpenter where you can build this picnic table and you can always look at and think about the hard work you put in and everything you crafted to make this," Meyer said.

The result is a distinctly local story; in addition to Straight to Ale's production equipment, the group purchased a keg washer from Good People. Working with local breweries has meant insight into how to best work with and maintain the equipment. The partners have been hands on in a number of building projects, and Meyer in particular has an aptitude for construction and repair.

"There is a lot of collaboration between the breweries," Andrew Pharo, who joined the team after Hayes left, told the *Birmingham Business Journal*. "We go to these events because all of the breweries get to hang out and talk and it's like a reunion. If someone needs ingredients, they can call us. It's such a grass roots effort and it is all just people that love what they do."

Although Cahaba's development came quickly, it wasn't without challenges. It's the only brewery in town where the owners maintain full-time jobs elsewhere.

"I say this a lot, but I think we have some of the most patient wives in the world," Meyer said.

The owners have little overhead because of low rent and few staff members; only two employees are full time. "We're not constrained on trying to get the beer out as fast as we can. We're not trying to put subpar beer into the market. And because of that, I think that has allowed us to continue on what we focused on…clean, consistent beer," Meyer explained.

Before those employees were brought on, the partners spent many late nights and weekends at the brewery, where even today some bottles are labeled by hand. The five-partner team has thirteen kids among them, and family is a priority. "I never wanted them to be like, 'Daddy was never here when I was a kid,'" said Gwaltney, who has spent many evenings at the brewery after he and his wife put their daughters to bed.

In June 2013, Gwaltney told *Birmingham* magazine that the brewery's biggest challenge was keeping up with demand. That year, Cahaba brewed 598 barrels, according to the *Birmingham Business Journal*. The partners give away 10 percent of the beer brewed each month for charitable causes and likewise must be selective about which requests they approve. Growth has remained steady; the brewery sold fifteen cases of 750ml bottles in August 2012 and, in January 2015, introduced cans of Cahaba Blonde Ale, which were contract brewed in Virginia. With time, the company has added more fermenters, employees and beer styles, an effort that will result in a 2015 move to a larger facility.

The former Continental Gin facility at 4500 Fifth Avenue South is fifty-one thousand square feet, which will allow room not only for Cahaba to introduce its own canning line but also for other businesses to share the building. In the early 1900s, the building housed the largest cotton gin–manufacturing company in the world.

"It would be great to try to revitalize that edge of Crestwood in Avondale and try to make it like a creative center. It's something I want to push," said Meyer, a firefighter. After all, brewing provides that sort of outlet for Cahaba's owners, sometimes in contrast to their day jobs. "It's just much more liberating to be creative," said Gwaltney, who works in telecommunications.

Cahaba Brewing's partners are excited by its role in the city but recognize that it's about more than beer—a key factor for the industry's continued growth. Dunn explained to the *Birmingham Business Journal* that breweries help attract young people, but it takes more than that to keep them in the city. "The real challenge we face in Birmingham is that the city needs more young professionals and more professional jobs to sustain this kind of growth," he said. "Right now, the reality is that the population growth is not great and we aren't adding those kind of jobs. I don't know how much impact we can have, but it's a challenge for Birmingham as a whole."

Even so, the breweries of the 2010s have seen signs that point to continued success, unlike that of their forefathers. "Most of us grew up watching Mr. Rogers, and we're used to go[ing] on to the candy factory and see[ing] how candy's made. We're used to go[ing] into this place and see[ing] how things were made, and that's why this generation wants to be local," Meyer said. "They want to see the stuff. They wanna be part of it because of how we are raised in that Mr. Rogers neighborhood."

The work of Free the Hops also changed the market, educating consumers and building demand for such products. "Consumers weren't ready for it back then," Meyer said, referring to the breweries and brewpubs of the '90s. "You also didn't have the quality standards that were held up. A lot of people back-talked about how, 'Oh, microbrew, that just tastes like home brew. My buddy did that back in college, and it suck[ed] then and still sucks today.'"

"I think the way we're going about it is a lot different, too," Gwaltney said. "I think the market is different. I think the way we went about it is different, too, because you know, we didn't jump into this, you know, that heavy and beholden to someone else."

10

RIGHT TO BREW

George Washington and Thomas Jefferson were both home brewers. President Barack Obama had a home brew setup at 1600 Pennsylvania Avenue. In 2013, the American Homebrewers Association estimated that there were one million home brewers in the country and about five thousand in Alabama. But the federally approved hobby was illegal in Alabama and Mississippi. (However, Alabama allowed for making up to five gallons of wine annually. The fruit used had to be grown on the property of a vintner.)

Home brewing had been on the rise for some time, with the American Brewers Association, in 1998, indicating that home brewing generated business of about $200 million annually, with associated retail growing at a rate of about 40 percent annually. Oversaturation ultimately led many suppliers into a survival, rather than growth, mode.

By 2009, the association had listed eight Alabama home brewing clubs. Alabama enforced its ban with some retail stores, but individuals were rarely caught—and when they were, extenuating factors were sometimes at play.

In 1994, Charles Baugh of the Alabama Alcoholic Beverage Control Board's enforcement division said to the *Birmingham News*, "Home brew is just like moonshine. It's illegal to make and illegal to possess." But he, too, said it was difficult to enforce because of other priorities, particularly illegal drugs, underage alcohol purchases and dry counties.

"Just like anything, if you do it at home, and you're not out selling it, and you're not making hundreds of gallons so your neighbors notice, we don't actively go after it," Alabama Alcoholic Beverage Control Board attorney Bob Martin told the Mobile *Press-Register*.

In 2010, Kade Miller, a resident of dry Blount County, was arrested during a raid on his home brewing setup, which authorities mistook for a hard liquor still. In 2013, a Mobile County prosecutor was disciplined for home brewing. He had regularly tweeted about his hobby. His boss, district attorney Ashley Rich, told the *Huntsville Times*, "We don't get to pick and choose the laws that we want to follow."

Business Interests

As interest in the state's beer laws grew, home brewing became part of the larger conversation. Atlanta-based Hop City Craft Beer & Wine opened its second location in Birmingham with the intent to include home brewing supplies as part of its wares. But before its 2012 opening, the Alcohol Beverage Control board confiscated $7,000 worth of equipment.

ABC attorney David Peacock said it was an inspection, not a raid, and that Hop City had been previously notified. He elaborated to the *Birmingham News*: "You can have sugar, you can have malt, you can have hops, you can have tubing, copper and everything else, but if you put it all together in a store and market it like it's going to be home brewing stuff and have a book about how to do it, it's a problem."

Owner Kraig Torres disagreed with Peacock's characterization of the event. "They've come into my store with three armed men and threatened to arrest my general manager on the grounds that we have supplies in the store that can be used to make beer," he told the paper.

Free the Hops prioritized ABV limit and container size over home brewing because of the greater economic ramifications of the two. Instead, the grass-roots lobbying organization Right to Brew led the way and began pushing a bill to legalize home brewing in 2011, when it received the Shroud Award for deadest bill. If passed, the bill would allow those of legal drinking age to brew up to fifteen gallons of beer, wine, mead or cider every three months, for personal use only. Those in dry counties or cities and felons would not be permitted to do so.

Endorsements rolled in. Birmingham Budweiser president Jay Dobbs issued a statement indicating that the bill would be good for Alabama business. In the *Huntsville Times*'s editorial section, Mike Hollis elaborated on reasons why the home brewing ban should be repealed:

> *Fifty years ago and before, it made sense for the state to have a law banning the sale and possession of the equipment and ingredients to make beer and wine to drink at home.*
>
> *At the time, the sale and possession of any sort of intoxicating drink or beverage was illegal in most Alabama counties, and sheriffs spent a lot of time and made a big to-do when they busted up moonshine stills deep in the piney woods.*
>
> *Times and attitudes change, and that's why the Legislature should repeal the law that bans the sale and possession of home beer brewing equipment and ingredients in cities and counties where alcohol isn't banned.*

In 2012, the bill passed the House after a four-plus-hour filibuster, but it failed to garner final approval before the session's end. In 2013, the battle resumed. It was one that advocates expected could take some time, in part because of the need for educating the public on who home brewers are.

"[Auburn attorney John] Little said that educating the public about home brewing is one of the most important steps needed to push the legalization of it. Many people think of home brewers as shady moonshiners, he said, when, in fact, most home brewers are middle-class citizens who look at brewing as a hobby," Dan Murtaugh wrote in the *Mobile Press-Register* in 2009. Little, who wrote a home brewing bill introduced that year, said to the paper, "It took Free the Hops four years. It may take us four years or longer."

Home brewer Jason Sledd spoke at a public hearing to the House Economic Development and Tourism Committee in February of that year. Sledd didn't realize the hobby was illegal when he had begun brewing the year prior. When Representative Berry Forte (D-Eufala) asked Sledd if he brewed in front of his kids, Sledd indicated that he did and used it as an opportunity to teach them responsibility and respect for the beverage. "They will have years of experience of seeing an adult drink alcohol and not being intoxicated," the *Birmingham News* reported Sledd as saying.

John J. Crowley Jr., in a 1997 letter to the *Huntsville Times*, wrote, "This May 3rd is National Homebrew Day. Homebrewing is a hobby enjoyed by millions throughout the United States and the world, except in locations where it is illegal such as Iraq, Iran, Kuwait, Saudi Arabia, Indonesia and Alabama. Have a nice National Homebrew Day."

But of course, opposition remained. Opponents argued that legalizing home brew would lead to alcohol abuse. "You're going to be setting a tone, not only in your home but in your area, that's going to entice others to drink," ALCAP executive director Joe Godfrey said. During 2013's debate in the House, he elaborated, "The bill encourages alcohol abuse and the many social problems that come with that. Home brewing can't be compared to other hobbies because alcohol can be addictive and dangerous."

Representative Arthur Payne (R-Trussville) seemed to agree with Godfrey. "We're just completely opening up the whole state to alcohol—every family, every home, every block. I represent a district that has a strong family unit, and we don't want to flood our neighborhoods with alcohol," the McClatchy Tribune quoted him as saying during the debate.

Bill sponsor Representative Mac McCutcheon (R-Huntsville) pushed back. The *Birmingham News* quoted him as saying, "This is about the rights of an individual to have the freedom to have a hobby that they enjoy…Drunkenness is a sin. Drunkenness is a result not of alcohol, but of the abuse of alcohol."

The arguments in defense of the Gourmet Beer Bill, Gourmet Bottle Bill and Brewery Modernization Act again applied to home brewing—and local media had occasionally written about them for years. "But home-brewers tend to seek good taste, not an exorbitant alcohol level," Shona Crabtree wrote in a 1995 *Press-Register* article. In a wire story published in the *Birmingham Post-Herald*, AHA director Jim Parker described home brewers as those willing to spend ten hours learning to make a drink worth five dollars.

"It's not cheap or easy. It takes four to five hours to brew a beer, and weeks more for that beer to be ready to drink. At $20 per batch for cheap homebrew ingredients, plus the cost of specialized brewing and bottling equipment, it's more economical for the would-be criminal to go to Walmart, buy a case of Natural Light and resell it, if that's their plan," wrote Dan Murphy, then an employee of the Mobile *Press-Register*. He later left the paper and became a partner at Fairhope Brewing in south Alabama.

Still others said that since the law wasn't enforced as it was, the legislature shouldn't spend time legalizing it. But spend the time it did. The governor signed the bill into law on May 9, 2013, making Alabama the forty-ninth state to legalize home brewing. (Mississippi passed its bill first, but it didn't take effect until July 1.)

After the senate passed the bill, according to the *Birmingham News*, Right to Brew posted on its site, "After a drama-filled day for us listening to the Senate, and after all hope seemed long lost, they brought up HB9 unexpectedly, out of the blue, and passed it 18-7-1 tonight, without a single word of debate. The Alabama Homebrew Bill has passed the Legislature!!!!"

WE BEAT MISSISSIPPI!

The *News*'s editorial following the bill's passage celebrated in jest beating Mississippi to the punch. The paper's Joey Kennedy, who wrote the editorial, also commended the legislators who shepherded the bill, noting that Jefferson County's delegation could learn from their cooperation.

Home brew competitions remain illegal, as home-brewed beers can't be sold or distributed to the public. "You could just drink your home-brew at home, but you'd be missing out on a large part of the community," James Spencer said to the McClatchy Tribune. Some states restrict such gatherings.

Even so, celebrations were notable. Birmingham Budweiser sponsored a home brewing competition to celebrate the Right to Brew law's passage. The contest was cosponsored by the American Homebrewers Association. "Many of the fine craft beers we distribute have their roots in home-brewing," Birmingham Budweiser president Jay Dobbs noted in a statement. The winner was Stott Noble's cream ale, which was then produced in a limited run at Cahaba Brewing Co.

"My business partners and I, we were just three guys who were home brewers, and yes, we learned our craft illegally. But we were able to find the equipment and grow. It's wonderful that home brewers in the state today can be open and honest about their passion," said Eric Meyer, managing partner at Cahaba Brewing Company. The brewery, in 2013, partnered with Hop City to create Unlock my Bock, a 6.5 percent ABV German bock. Some proceeds went to Right to Brew. Cahaba Brewing's founders were home brewers, and the beer was sold at both sites.

Cigar City Brewing began selling its beers in Alabama again in October 2013, and one of the selections was Wiregrass Post-Prohibition Ale, which celebrated the state's passage of its home brew bill. Cigar City brewmaster Wayne Wambles is an Alabama native, and the brewery had briefly sold its beer in Alabama two years earlier.

The economic impact of the bill was quickly visible. Auburn University, a two-hour drive from Birmingham, launched a brewing program in 2014. Hop City saw a 15 percent increase in business after the bill passed. "Trying to operate without that 15 percent for the last 10 months has been a challenge. But now we're teaching home-brew classes on Saturday, and things are booming," home brew manager Spencer Overton told the *Birmingham News*. He said the city was now on the cutting edge of the craft beer scene: "As breweries around the state begin to grow, Birmingham is going to become known as a place where beer is part of the culture, like Asheville, North Carolina, or Boulder, Colorado." However, if the bill hadn't passed, he was concerned his job at Hop City wouldn't last.

Craft brewing remained a growing trend nationwide; months after the home brewing bill's passage, a report from IBISWorld indicated that the craft brewing industry had grown nationally at a rate of 10.9 percent in the previous five years. The report also suggested that growth should slow to 7.2 percent in the next five but that those figures might look different in Alabama and other southern states. With Alabama and some of its neighbors playing catch-up because of previously restrictive beer laws, the market could continue to boom. The South represents a quarter of the country's population but at that time accounted for just 12 percent of American breweries.

"It took Free the Hops a long time to get people to realize that just because you liked beer didn't mean you were out to destroy the state," Free the Hops's Gabe Harris said. But by 2013, with major legislative changes secured, public opinion differed. "Everybody's kind of come around to our side."

II

TRIM TAB BREWING CO.

It started with a dream. Engineer Buckminster Fuller appeared to Harris Stewart as if in a prophecy. Fuller often correlated the trim tab, a small rudder used to steer a ship, with human capacity for affecting change. By acting within one's sphere of influence, Fuller said, a single person could create lasting ripples. "It's basically the physical embodiment of a small source of big change," Harris explained.

When Harris awoke on that July 2011 morning, the future was clear: he would open Trim Tab Brewing Co.

"Why can't we use craft beer as a way to spread that universal idea and to inspire people into action to do more with their sphere of influence and to use our space as a way to create or strengthen, magnify community groups that may be doing amazing things but don't get enough attention?" wondered Harris, then a student at the University of Alabama School of Law.

"I'm not going to be a trim tab if I follow the path I'm on," Cheri Stewart recalled her husband saying.

The Stewarts had long daydreamed about opening a brewery. The couple met while enrolled at the University of North Carolina–Asheville and would often head to Wedge Brewing to drink and discuss. Although there were a number of art studios in the neighborhood prior to the brewery, Wedge's popularity ensured that people came to the district to support those artists.

"It was a place you could go to by yourself or with friends, read by yourself or meet someone cool. We just loved the community feel of it," said Cheri, who attended the North Carolina School of the Arts and went to college in

Trim Tab Brewing owners Harris and Cheri Stewart dressed in style for the brewery's Bootleggers Ball. *Brad Lovell Photography.*

Asheville because of its hippie vibe. "We saw the power a brewery had to bring people together around fun—not this serious thing, like church or even yoga, but a fun thing."

The couple began daydreaming about combining their love of beer and community in a brewery.

"For us, beer is more than beer. It has a force for bringing people together," said Harris, who began home brewing while the couple lived in Asheville. "It's a medium for people sharing experiences together. Craft beer, in particular, has always been at its best when it tells a really compelling narrative, when it tells a story."

But the dream seemed farfetched. The couple decided to pursue careers elsewhere, intending to save money until opening a brewery looked feasible. After a stint in finance, though, Cheri realized it wasn't for her. Harris's career in solar energy became less fulfilling after an ownership change at work, so he decided to follow a path well worn by his family. The Stewarts relocated to Tuscaloosa, Alabama, where Harris enrolled in the University of Alabama School of Law and Cheri taught yoga.

The Tuscaloosa yoga scene wasn't strong, though, so Cheri was under a lot of pressure to make every class work. When she learned that yoga clothing retailer Lululemon was opening a store an hour away in Birmingham, possibility loomed. She became a manager, which offered a steady paycheck and allowed her yoga classes to be more relaxed rather than a means of supporting the couple.

On the other hand, Harris was successful but unsatisfied with law school, and he also brewed at home three times a week. "It was like part of his soul was slowly dying. He was not fulfilled or happy and not inspired by the possibility of where he was going in his future," Cheri said.

That's when Bucky came in. Even though he still didn't think it was an immediate possibility, Harris began drafting a business plan for Trim Tab Brewing Co. and soon filed articles of incorporation.

"It was more a question of when, not if, we are going to be able to make this happen," he said.

Dinner with Cheri's manager led to the next step. "I don't see you being a lawyer," manager Kelly Bohnet said to Harris. "Why don't you just try to do this now?" And so, the Stewarts began speaking to investors, located the property and launched the business.

It was the Lululemon philosophy embodied, Cheri said. "Part of the culture of Lululemon is this goal-setting culture. Lululemon teaches this philosophy that is so inspiring, a transformational way of looking at the world, which is limitless, dwelling in a world of possibility."

The couple began looking for investors and a location when they found a contest run by Birmingham's Barber Companies. The company began promoting the giveaway of a piece of property across from downtown's City Federal Building about 2009. George Barber offered it free to anyone with a solid business plan and financing, but after three years, inquiries dried up.

Stewart's post-college experience at a startup offered insight into the challenges ahead. But when Harris decided to apply for the Barber contest, he learned entrepreneurship by fire. Within weeks, he had compiled a business plan and secured the property.

In May 2012, the company announced a deal with Trim Tab Brewing. At the time, Harris was a third-year student at the University of Alabama School of Law. Trim Tab was originally to include a hot chicken restaurant, and Stewart intended it to include multiple stories, with a rooftop bar.

"It was like an incubator. It was a place I could start to talk to people about. I could bring them to the site. I could breathe life into words that were at that point just on a page. That is where I started to really drum up interest," he said.

The owners spent two years raising the initial investment while beginning to build their staff.

Although Harris was a home brewer, he didn't intend to be Trim Tab's brewmaster. "I was really wanting to build a team of people who bought into the vision and then we could magnify each other's specialties to a cohesive whole," he said. So the Stewarts placed a national ad and encountered Will Crenshaw.

Crenshaw, a graduate of the University of California–Davis's master brewers program, also passed the nine-hour Institute of Brewers and Distilling Examination. He's the first Alabama brewer to have completed the program. He received a bachelor's in biology from Birmingham-Southern College and earned a master's in biochemistry from the University of Tennessee. His interest in craft beer developed in grad school.

During two and a half years at Sweetwater Brewing Co. in Atlanta, Crenshaw saw the output grow from 65,000 to 100,000 barrels a year. He was attracted to Trim Tab because of the opportunity to have more control over the process and recipes, he told the *Birmingham News*. "Say, one brewery does a really great IPA or double IPA or something that like that, we're not going to try to do one better on that. We really want to bring in different beer styles that are underrepresented there," he said.

"With all our beers, we're trying to specialize in balanced complexity, we say, which for us means having a lot of depth of flavor, a lot of complexity," Harris said. Living in the South, where summers often creep into the one-hundred-degree range, also meant a need for beers with lower alcohol content, often called session beers because several can be safely consumed in a single sitting.

The brewery received its equipment in September 2013, giving it the capacity to brew 3,500 kegs annually. The space is large enough to brew as much as sixty thousand barrels a year, though, allowing room to grow.

Harris said Crenshaw's hiring meant a change in expectations. His new brewmaster was capable of great things, and he no longer believed the small downtown property would be sufficient for Trim Tab's growth. And so Harris returned to Barber Companies in search of something different. The men at the board table listened and quickly brought him to another facility: 2721 Fifth Avenue South, the former home of the Barber Motorsports Museum and a building that had sat vacant for years.

Cheri took the lead on designing the space while Harris continued raising money and focusing on the business's finances. Money was limited, so Cheri knew she would have to get creative in the former car museum. "The industrial spaces are actually kind of easy to do that if you don't fight the space but you see the beauty in it, you bring it out," she said.

Elements of the design came together organically; through a friend, the couple learned about Upcycle Birmingham, a family-owned business

Trim Tab Brewing's taproom has hosted a variety of events, including the popular TEDxBirmingham salons. *Brad Lovell Photography.*

that repurposes old wood. The company made the main bar, back bar and the bars that line the tasting gallery's walls for what Cheri describes as a "ridiculously low price." Cheri selected white walls because she knew the space, once a car print shop, would double as an art gallery.

"I wanted the space to always be changing and be different because our vision statement is 'elevating culture through craft beer.' Part of that is having the space around you be inspiring for our guests," she said. "[The art] can completely transform the space. The show before this was a photography show, and it was really minimal. It made it feel a lot more austere in here, but it was cool for a while."

With those decisions set, she filled in with modern touches, such as IKEA furniture, and saved money by purchasing stools and rugs on Overstock.com.

The taproom is an essential part of the brewery's success, Harris said, and a distinction that has made today's breweries successful when the '90s forefathers were not. "This is where people come to learn and communicate and eventually thrive with a brand they've developed a deep, personal relationship with," he explained.

Cheri handles the artist booking, and each show lasts two to three months, depending on how much the work excites her. The brewery doesn't take a gallery fee. "We want to enable people to have fun while being inspired in their lives," Harris said.

That philosophy applies to hiring, as well. Every employee goes through at least three interviews and must attend monthly staff meetings. Each meeting includes discussion of required reading, typically from personal development books. Cheri plans questions intended to spur discussion about how the team can continue to develop. "It's really a lot of open communication and valuing the opinions of my employees and empowering them to take ownership of the business," she said.

In March 2014, the brewery hired the area's first female brewer, Lauren Wiersma. She was previously employed at Oskar Blues Brewing and Left Hand Brewing, both based in Longmont, Colorado. Wiersma grew up in Vestavia Hills and attended Birmingham-Southern College; a desire for warm weather drew her back home.

"His business plan was the best I had seen so far, and it was the kind of company I wanted to work with," Wiersma told the *Birmingham News*. She interviewed over beers when she and Stewart happened to be in New Orleans at the same time.

Trim Tab has high expectations for its employees, but those result in high levels of trust. On the taproom's second weekend in business, the Stewarts left town for a half marathon and entrusted the bar to three employees. "We expect more, but if you give and you take ownership of this company, we're going to reward you. We take care of our people," Cheri said, indicating a starting wage higher than most bartending positions and opportunities for raises based on Cicerone certification. A number of bartenders have already been promoted to other positions, such as tour leader, sales representative, office manager, event planner and assistant manager.

Cheri loves beer, but it's not her driving force. "People are my passion," she said. Cheri credits her experience at Lululemon in part for her understanding the power of managing people. "You have the power to create jobs for people to live lives that they love and become leaders. Whether they stay with you or they go off and do something amazing, that's so fulfilling and incredible."

"We knew the type of communication we wanted to stand for with our people and the type of environment we wanted to create for our employees," Cheri said.

"That is the brand made complete manifest," Harris said. "From the very beginning, Cheri always understood that to be of the highest importance."

Following a 2013 Magic City Brewfest premiere, Trim Tab opened its tasting gallery in February 2014, with art by Paul Cordes Wilm on display. It accounted for two thousand square feet in the fourteen-thousand-square-foot building. The company brewed its first commercial batch in January of that year, with several beers offering nods to the city's English heritage.

Pillar to Post Brown Ale was the first beer brewed in the space and plays on an English phrase that means something is unnecessarily difficult. In this case, it's a nod to Trim Tab's lengthy journey, which began nearly three years before things took off. "We've got to tip our hats at least somewhat to the epic odyssey it took to get there," Harris said. It was one of two Trim Tab beers that entered the final round of judging at the 2014 Great American Beer Fest. The summer seasonal Raspberry Weiss was also in the running.

In its first year, the tasting gallery quickly became a place for revolutionary conversations, including TEDxBirmingham's quarterly salons.

"One of the beautiful things that beer does is it raises spirits," Harris said. "It gets people to sit and maybe perhaps speak a little bit more boldly than they would, express opinions or ideas that they might be too inhibited otherwise to really express." The brewery also gained additional business as attendees began booking the venue for events.

By the time Trim Tab launched, Alabama's beer industry had doubled in size for each of the three previous years, and the Alabama Brewers Guild expected the brewing industry to double again in 2013. It projected that the state would produce 38,944 barrels in 2013—a projection only slightly higher than reality, as state brewers churned out 32,531 barrels of beer.

Trim Tab's growth has been on par, with its first expansion announced in early 2015. The brewery expects to begin canning its beers before the end of the year.

"We want to get our beer in cans and then in stores so eventually this Trim Tab philosophy and culture slowly gets spread to people sitting on their couch, reading the back of a can," Cheri said.

Long term, the couple dreams of opening additional locations. Cheri hopes to eventually hand management off to her assistant manager so she can focus on human resources and raising a family. The possibilities seem limitless—which is why the couple was attracted to Birmingham.

"I just noticed so many young people who had good jobs and were making shit happen," Cheri said, noting that it wasn't the same back home. "This is a place where young people are supported and respected as entrepreneurs and people who can make something happen. We saw possibility, and that's why we decided on Birmingham."

12

GOOD PEOPLE GROWING

As the state's legislative landscape changed, Birmingham's oldest brewery aimed to grow a specific demographic through its educational arm. Hops for Honeys, a women's craft beer club, formed in 2010 and drew inspiration from a similar organization at Colorado's Left Hand Brewing Co. Michael Sellers's wife, Melinda, and Jason Malone's wife, Kerri, organized the first meeting of the craft beer education group in May 2010.

"My motive is selfish, right? I'm supporting my family by marketing an area that is not typically marketed to women," Sellers told *Paste* magazine. "Women are seen as wine and cocktail drinkers, and we're a huge part of the population. It's silly for beer companies not to capitalize on that." Sellers is also a certified Cicerone and in her work as an attorney often works with distributors and brewers.

Continued exponential growth resulted in Good People's move to a larger facility less than two years after selling its first beer. It moved into a twenty-five-thousand-square-foot facility adjacent to Railroad Park in May 2010, four months before the park opened. In 2009, the *Birmingham Business Journal* identified the park as a project that could transform downtown, and indeed the brewery saw the neighborhood take off. The move to a larger space allowed for bigger, and more, brewing equipment, including a canning line. In March 2011, Good People IPA and brown ale debuted in six packs.

"There's been a lot of talk around town about how fast Good People Brewing Co.'s first run of canned beer disappeared from store shelves.

Good People also encourages beer education through Hops for Honeys, its women's craft beer group. *Gabe Harris.*

However fast you heard it went, it went faster than that. On the Friday that it was first shipped, Birmingham Beverage distributed six hundred cases of the beer to ten retail establishments," said Jack Davis, area sales manager for the beer distributor.

"Most of that beer was gone within five hours of the time it hit the shelves," *Birmingham News*'s Roy Williams wrote. Weeks later, the beer was still in heavy demand, with the IPA outselling the brown. In the years that followed, the company added its Snakehandler double IPA, pale ale and coffee oatmeal stout—which quickly became its second most popular—to the canning lineup. Each bears the label "legally brewed since 2008," a nod to the company's home brewing origins.

AlaBev's Matt Kilpatrick described the state's beer popularity to the *Birmingham Business Journal*. "If you look at unbiased scanned items from grocery stores, the number one selling craft beer is Good People IPA," he said. "The guerrilla marketing effort, I guess, was just right for the state of Alabama. I think the territorial nature of the Alabamian is the reason for that. We're so local anyway. Look at college football or anything else

Good People's Snakehandler, a double IPA, was the only Birmingham beer on *Men's Journal*'s 101 Best Beers in America list in 2015. *Gabe Harris.*

that comes from the state of Alabama. People are always first in line to put their hands on it. Beer just fit right into that perfect demographic."

After the Brewery Modernization Act passed in 2011, Good People opened a taproom, and it quickly became a hit. It allowed for tastes and tours—and even if you opted out of a formal tour, you would drink within sight of where the beer was brewed.

"It's one of the best things to happen to the beer industry in Alabama for a long time," Sellers told the *Mobile Press-Register*. "You get people in, you can educate people on beer, get your name out there."

At the time, the taproom was the sole form of entertainment adjacent to Railroad Park. The neighborhood drastically changed in 2013, when Regions Field opened across the street from the brewery. It was a stroke of luck that almost went awry; at one point, the brewery's property was a possibility for the ballpark's location. Even with expanded traffic to the facility, Sellers said he didn't think the property would change much. "We are a manufacturer first and foremost," he told the *Birmingham News*.

"As much as I love baseball and as much as I love having the ballpark downtown, if it did not have the potential to generate the economic development interest, it would not have interested me as the mayor of the

Good People beers represent a variety of styles. Alcohol by volume, standard reference method and international bitterness units help consumers know what to expect of each beer. *Paul MacWilliams.*

city," Bell said to the *News* prior to the park's opening. "We see this as being a strong driver to build that bridge between UAB and downtown and attract people from all over the region."

The area became an example for the city. John Archibald of the *Birmingham News* wrote, "Birmingham has even become a city of spirits, if you can believe it. Good People Brewing Company and Avondale Brewing Company have created a whole bunch of beer buzz. And maybe, when you get right down to it, it was the beer folks who came closest to telling the world exactly what this city is all about. Birmingham is good people."

Before Good People opened, the owners told the *Birmingham Business Journal* they didn't expect to exceed two thousand barrels a year in what they foresaw to be a small operation. Plans change. By 2011, when Olde Town closed, Good People was left as the state's oldest brewery. It was three years old. Rapid growth soon made Good People the state's largest brewery, as well.

The company regularly increased its capacity and, in 2013, produced 8,500 barrels of beer. That year, the brewery also added a pub at Birmingham-Shuttlesworth International Airport and expanded distribution to Nashville. Sellers told the *Birmingham Business Journal* that he hoped the brewery would eventually have a twelve- to fifteen-state footprint.

"When we first walked in here, we thought we could grow to the size of Budweiser and never need more space. Now we've realized that's not the case," Malone said in July 2014, promising that the brewery would look dramatically different within a year. In February 2015, it temporarily closed for renovations. Planned changes included a new patio, a glass wall separating the tasting area from the brewery and air conditioning in the taproom—a first.

"We wanted to invest in this side of town, the Parkside area," Sellers told the *Birmingham News*. "As the anchor over here, we wanted to keep up our end of the deal and put our best foot forward for this area."

The sixteen-thousand-square-foot brewery made its mark on the local industry, with twelve employees hired by 2014, according to a Google report. And although Google noted the brewery's success because of its social media campaigns, others lauded the beer itself. In 2014, it was one of five Birmingham bars listed on *Southern Living*'s list of the one hundred best in the South, and the magazine also named Good People's IPA its favorite craft beer from Alabama. Likewise, in 2013, the website Thrillist identified Good People as Alabama's best-known alcohol purveyor, and in 2015 the site included Good People in its best breweries in America March Madness bracket. (The eleventh-seeded brewery made the elite eight.)

Still, the owners' hands-on involvement remains crucial, as it does at other area breweries, said Trim Tab Brewing owner Harris Stewart. "Jason and Michael, they're there at the brewery all the time. All the breweries—they're there," Harris said. "The people who own the brewery, they're there. It's not some corporation. You can talk to people and they give you all this feedback."

Sellers and Malone credit their success largely to their simple love of beer. "I think what makes us unique is we are a definite beer-driven brewery, always have been, since day one. There wasn't opportunity then. We were probably naïve about it," Sellers said with a laugh. "It wasn't like craft beer was in the paper. Wanting to do it was driven by…we love this style of beer, this craft beer, this artisan product. It's a sense of pride for us, knowing that beer was the catalyst, not opportunity."

13
BIRMINGHAM BREWING, THE ECONOMY AND THE FUTURE

Years of hard work, largely contributed by volunteers of Free the Hops and Right to Brew, as well as beer industry employees, resulted in a changed Birmingham beer landscape. When Free the Hops began in 2005, the city was home to a few bottle shops, a handful of sports bars with a decent beer selection and zero breweries.

Ten years later, options abound.

Tampa-based beer bar chain World of Beer opened a Birmingham location in 2012, offering forty beers on tap and as many as six hundred bottles.

"It's a great opportunity to be coming into Alabama, just because of the [beer] movement and all the change in laws that haven't been changed for many years," said Rayford Cook, operations manager and vice-president for the company that planned multiple Alabama locations. He believed there was room for both World of Beer and the J. Clyde. "Business brings business and awareness to our movement in craft beers," he told the *Birmingham News*.

Hop City, the craft beer and wine store that saw its home brew equipment seized in 2012, has experienced continual growth. The 5,500-square-foot shop added a covered patio in 2013 because on-site consumption proved more popular than expected. The tasting area was intended to allow people to sample beers while deciding what to buy but has resonated so much that people treat it like a bar. But the store wouldn't have been possible prior to changes in Alabama's ABV and container size laws.

"With the laws [the way] they were, you wouldn't be offering that much. You wouldn't be offering 1,200 beers, you'd be offering 200 beers," said Josh Terrell.

Also that year, a music, beer and wine festival was launched in the shop's Lakeview neighborhood. Cask & Drum capitalized in part on the craft beer scene while highlighting the area in which it was held.

Economic Development

"Free the Hops was the key. That opened the door. There's no doubt about that," said Steve Betts of the 1990s' Birmingham Brewing. "Then the legislation changed to raise the alcohol limits where they could brew these styles."

As proponents promised, the economic impact has been substantial. Birmingham Budweiser president Jay Dobbs wrote in the *Birmingham Business Journal* that the breweries have been catalysts for economic development in their neighborhoods. Good People's Sellers has cautioned that the beer revolution's influence can be overhyped, but it has played a role in the city's recent development.

"It has spurred cleanup and growth in Avondale," Sellers said. "It has spurred cleanup and growth around Railroad Park—maybe not spurred but contributed. You've got your guys over at Trim Tab. It's almost like that U.S. 78 corridor that's coming through downtown—no longer is there a dark area between I-65 and I-20/59. I think the beer has become anchor points that things can be built around."

Trim Tab's Stewart pointed to a number of possible reasons:

> I think maybe because Alabama has such an inferiority complex relative to a lot of states that the beer in Birmingham, the beer in Alabama, people take ownership of it. They live in the Avondale area, or they live near Good People downtown, or just live in Birmingham in general, they're going to have some ownership of those breweries because it's something they can be proud of. It's something that [when] people come from out of state and visit them, they can say, let's go to Good People, let's go to this great brewery and have a lot of fun there. Because of that, people will go there, that helps out all the stuff around the brewery.

Danner Kline told *Business Alabama*:

> The increase in craft beers has been going on nationally for more than a decade, and it's the changes in our laws in Alabama that has allowed it

to flourish here. It ties into the local, slow-food and organic movements. The Millennial generation is more interested in something they can feel a connection to, that they feel is genuine and has a story, rather than a corporate brand.

The Stewarts saw that change when they lived in North Carolina and believe it could be a model for what awaits Birmingham. "There's this real tipping point that we saw in Asheville, and I think we've seen it a lot of other places where beer has really become adopted with the local, civic identity. It starts to become a part of the lifestyle of living there. There's this tipping point when there is enough of it around, people stop viewing it as a novelty. It starts to accelerate on each other, and it deeply affects the culture of the place that's there," Harris Stewart said.

Betts and his wife, Pat, agree that the homegrown aspect remains appealing. "The craft industry isn't just beer. It's food. It's art. It's all kinds of things. Beer is all that rolled into one thing. That was the part that intrigued me about the business," he said. And the craft segment's appeal to younger people in particular has galvanized change. "The old is dying out," Pat Betts said. "The young is taking over."

But the more important effort, Stewart noted, is growing the market share as a whole. Craft beer represents 7.8 percent of the beer market nationally. Even as total beer sales have declined, craft beer sales have been on the rise. Craft beer saw a 17.2 percent increase in 2013, according to the Brewers Association.

Jerry Hartley at the J. Clyde acknowledges that the introduction of taprooms has affected his pub's business, but he also adheres to the adage "a rising tide lifts all ships." Hartley said he, too, is drawn to consuming beer at its source and hopes the craft beer market share continues to grow—to every business's benefit.

The market growth has been a boon for brewers outside of the state, as well. SweetWater Brewing Co. marketing director Steve Farce said to the Associated Press, "The craft community of beer drinkers is growing, so therefore sales for all craft beer are growing at a double-digit rate. So there's plenty of room for lots more craft breweries to come online." SweetWater's Alabama sales have increased during the more than ten years it's been for sale in Alabama.

As of late 2013, Alabama Brewers Guild president Jason Wilson noted that Alabama-brewed beer accounted for no more than 2 percent of state beer sales. "We're all about growing that piece of the pie," Stewart said.

FUTURE OPPORTUNITY

But it's difficult to compare Birmingham's potential to the success of other southern markets, such as Nashville and Asheville, North Carolina, both of which have well-developed tourism draws. "At some point, whether you're opening a new brewery, a new bar, a new restaurant—forget beer, just a restaurant—you're sort of chasing the same wallets," Good People's Malone said. Sales outside of the state represent growth opportunity, but the brewery's Sellers agreed with his business partner, noting Alabama's 4.8 million population as a limiting factor. "We have a limited market just by demographics," he told the Associated Press.

Craft beer plays a role in quality of life, which can help draw more industry to Birmingham. The overall scene's growth is dependent in part on the population of consumers growing.

Good People's Sellers echoed that sentiment:

> *Obviously, though, you have to be concerned or you have to be aware that taprooms take up a portion of the entertainment dollar or the drinking dollar out of the community. When we have a big crowd or Avondale has a big crowd or whoever has a big crowd, that's a big crowd that's not at the J. Clyde, not here, not at Carrigan's, not at Rogue. When people say Birmingham can handle all these, I'm like, Birmingham needs jobs. Birmingham needs population boost. We need Honda to open up a place in Gardendale. That's what we need. Right now we're just transferring dollars from Hoover in.*
>
> *This has been a very good economic lesson for us, that you see how all these dollars shift. Birmingham doesn't really have more revenue. They're just shifting that revenue around to different areas of town.*

Even so, Alabama beer's economic impact has steadily grown. In 2014, craft beer in Alabama was at 32,531 barrels (thirty-ninth in the nation) and had a $238.1 million economic impact (fiftieth in the nation), according to the Brewers Association. The organization's economist told AL.com that if Alabama were to reach the averages in economic and employment per capita, the state could add $284 million to the gross domestic product and three thousand related jobs (direct, indirect and induced).

The existing numbers grow when including associated businesses. According to a 2013 study conducted by the Center for Applied Business & Economic Research at the University of Delaware and commissioned by

National Beer Wholesalers Association, Alabama beer distributors account, directly or not, for more than eight thousand jobs and an annual economic impact of $733 million.

In June 2014, the nation broke the three-thousand-brewery mark for the first time since the 1870s, and those involved in the industry believe Alabama is poised for similar continued growth. "The more the industry grows here, it's better for all of us as a whole. I think Birmingham and Alabama in general has the potential to create many more breweries and all of us be successful," Coby Lake told the *Birmingham News* in 2010.

And although Kline has cautioned that the number of breweries might eventually exceed demand, Back Forty and Alabama Brewers Guild's Jason Wilson believes that's in the distant future.

"For a long time after Prohibition, beer was seen as a very generic product in this country. Every other thing that American consumers buy, they demand options. But for so long, the exception to that rule was beer. Now Americans are looking at the beer aisle the way they look at every other aisle. So I think it's premature to say that we're reaching some sort of saturation point," Wilson said to *Business Alabama*.

As of March 2015, the Alabama Brewers Guild included twenty-six brewing members, and plans for new breweries and brewpubs were often announced.

"Alabama has been the fastest-growing state in regards to the number of breweries that have opened in the last year, and I don't see this slowing down anytime soon. I do know that the amount of beer produced in Alabama and the number of employees at our craft brewers are expected to double in 2013 from where they were in 2012. This can only be good for the state," Free the Hops's Gabe Harris told the *Birmingham News* in 2013.

The Way Forward

Although Free the Hops has concluded its legislative agenda, opportunities for change remain. Alabama and Georgia are the only states that prohibit off-premise brewery sales. Breweries can sell beer by the glass, but growlers or six-packs for take-home consumption are illegal. The Alabama Brewers Guild is pushing for that change in the 2015 legislative session, and it could introduce an additional revenue stream for breweries.

That sort of deregulation could also open up the state to the country's major macrobrewers. "Do we want Budweiser to come build a brewery here?

Maybe! If they hire twenty thousand people, that might be something," Sellers said.

Additional breweries could add to the economy, but the Alabama legislative environment is still limiting. Tampa's Cigar City Brewing is currently exploring options for a second brewery outside Florida, but founder Joey Redner said Alabama isn't of interest.

"Favorable laws that allow direct on-site sales and self-distribution are, I am convinced, pivotal to the financial and marketing success of a small brewery," he told the *Huntsville Times*. The state's three-tier system prohibits self-distribution.

"The same reasons that they're not interested in coming here are the same reasons our breweries are going to have a hard time really thriving in the national market," Alabama Brewers Guild executive director Dan Roberts said to the *Huntsville Times*.

In March 2015, the Alabama Brewers Guild also introduced a bill that would give breweries opportunities to change the wholesale distributors with which they work. Existing laws would not allow such a change when breweries were dissatisfied with their distributors.

Free the Hops has always been a consumer organization, so founder Danner Kline and other board members have determined that the best way to defend a consumer's interest is to support the brewers guild's efforts. He said, "At this point, anything that the brewers guild is trying to do is going to be a net benefit for the consumer, and they have the business clout and the economic data to back up whatever they want to do."

Work may remain, but opportunity reigns. "In a lot of ways, the South has trailed the development of the rest of the country," Harris Stewart said, "but a beautiful thing right now in these is the fact that it isn't as saturated as other places. There's so much room for creativity and growth."

In a city with a history of responding to the ingenuity of its brewers and other artisans, the possibilities seem endless.

BIBLIOGRAPHY

BOOKS

Bull, Donald, Manfred Friedrich and Robert Gottschalk. *American Breweries*. Trumbull, CT: Bullworks, 1984.

McMillan, Malcolm C. *Yesterday's Birmingham*. Miami, FL: E.A. Seemann Publishing, 1975.

Nachel, Marty, and Steve Ettlinger. *Beer for Dummies*. Foster City, CA: IDG Books, 1996.

Oliver, Garrett. *The Brewmaster's Table*. New York: Ecco, 2003.

Oliver, Garrett, ed. *The Oxford Companion to Beer*. New York: Oxford University Press, 2012.

One Hundred Years of Brewing: A Complete History of the Progress Made in Art, Science and Industry of Brewing in the World, Particularly During the Last Century. Chicago: H.S. Rich & Company, 1901.

Sellers, James Benson. *The Prohibition Movement in Alabama, 1702 to 1943*. Chapel Hill: University of North Carolina Press, 1943.

United States Internal Revenue Service. *Annual Report*. Commissioner of Internal Revenue, 1908.

INTERVIEWS BY THE AUTHOR

Betts, Steve. Urban Standard, February 4, 2015.

Harris, Gabe. The J. Clyde, November 11, 2014.

Hartley, Jerry. The J. Clyde, January 8, 2015.

Kline, Danner. The J. Clyde, June 3, 2014.

Bibliography

Lake, Coby, and Hunter Lake. Avondale Brewing Co., October 13, 2014.

Malone, Jason. Good People Brewing Co., July 16, 2014.

Meyer, Eric, and Andy Gwaltney. Cahaba Brewing Co., February 17, 2015.

Sellers, Melinda. Trattoria Centrale, July 29, 2014.

Sellers, Michael. Iron City Birmingham, July 22, 2014.

Stewart, Cheri. Trim Tab Brewing Co., February 5, 2015.

Stewart, Harris. Trim Tab Brewing Co., January 15, 2015.

Terrell, Josh. Hop City Craft Beer and Wine, March 3, 2015.

Magazines and Newspapers

Aaron, Haley. "On Tap: New Beer Law Boosts City Bar Coffers." *Birmingham Business Journal*, July 12, 2009.

Alexander, Alan. "More of a Whiskey State? Alabama Ranks 22nd for Beer Consumption." *Birmingham Business Journal*, July 3, 2013.

———. "Why Trouble Is Not Brewing in Bham's Beer Scene." *Birmingham Business Journal*, December 13, 2013.

Altman, George R. "Committee Passes Free the Hops Bill." *Mobile Register*, February 19, 2009.

Amy, Jeff. "Mobile Brewpub Weathers Shutdown of Sister Site." *Mobile Register*, June 21, 2000.

Anderson, Jon. "Brewery Adding Another Storage Tank." *Birmingham News*, February 4, 1994.

Anniston Star. "Ready to Try a Specialty Brew? Here's Where to Find Alabama Pubs." November 12, 1995.

Archibald, John. "Birmingham Has Its Own Flavor of Good People." *Birmingham News*, January 6, 2012.

———. "Brewmaster Taps Education to Put a Head on 'Pensive' Ale." *Birmingham News*, October 18, 1996.

———. "Don't Put Legislature on Scales." *Birmingham News*, May 22, 2008.

Associated Press. "Beer Bill Wins Shroud Award." *Birmingham News*, June 8, 2007.

———. "A Beer Revolution Is Brewing in Alabama." *Birmingham News*, December 29, 2013.

———. "Beer Tasting Course Is for the 'Stout' Hearted." *Mobile Register*, August 31, 1994.

———. "Birmingham Brewmaster Reopening Old Brewery." *Gadsden Times*, February 22, 1992.

———. "Birmingham Gets Brew Pub: Owner of Mobile's Port City Brewery Expands with Magic City Brewery." *Mobile Register*, March 11, 1995.

———. "Free the Hops Seeks Looser Beer Restrictions." *Huntsville Times*, October 30, 2007.

————. "Group Wants to Raise State Alcohol Amount, Size Limit for Beer." *Birmingham News*, October 30, 2007.

————. "Home Brew Bill Gets Closer." *Birmingham News*, May 9, 2012.

————. "Lawmaker Targets Liquor Board." *Huntsville Times*, January 17, 1993.

————. "Storm Brewing in Legislature on Beer Strength." *Birmingham News*, May 30, 1995.

Azok, Dawn Kent. "Birmingham's New Trim Tab Brewing Co. Aims to Build Culture, Owner Says." *Birmingham News*, February 14, 2014.

Bagwell, Dan. "Ranked: Alabama's Top Breweries." *Birmingham Business Journal*, November 24, 2014.

Ball, Mays S. "Alabama's Fierce Struggle Over Prohibition." *Frank Leslie's Weekly*, December 30, 1909.

Beasley, Cecil. "Elephant No Prohibitionist Especially When Sick, Trainer Declares." Birmingham Public Library Digital Collections. http://bplonline.cdmhost.com/cdm/search/searchterm/Parks.

Berry, Lucy. "Alabama Ranks 50th in Per-Capita Economic Beer Impact; Policy Makers Must Remove Manufacturing Barriers to Support Growth." AL.com, February 11, 2015.

————. "Brewers Guild Fights to Pass Bill to Make Wholesale Beer Contracts Enforceable in Alabama." AL.com, March 26, 2015.

————. "Cheers to Beer Growth Craft Brews: Alabama Breweries Welcome Consumers' 'Unquenchable' Thirst for Local Products." *Huntsville Times*, September 21, 2014.

————. "Craft Brewers Tapping State to Change Law Distribution Change: Alabama Brewers Want State to Allow Direct Sales of Craft Beers." *Huntsville Times*, December 3, 2014.

————. "2 Alabama Craft Brews Make 101 Best Beers in America List." AL.com, March 27, 2015.

Birmingham Age. "German Mardi Gras." March 9, 1886.

Birmingham Business Journal. "Alabama Ranks 22nd for Beer Consumption." October 15, 2012.

————. "Avondale Brewing to Launch Canned Beer Line." October 17, 2014.

————. "Beer Engineers Plans Brewery near Railroad Park." April 16, 2013.

————. "Brewing in Five Points." January 20, 2008.

————. "Cheers! Craft Brewers Outpace Big Beer Production." March 4, 2014.

————. "Entrepreneur Spotlight—Good People Brewing Co." August 24, 2012.

Birmingham News. "All's Not So Well That Ends Not So Well." April 25, 2010.

————. "Brewers of Beer: Brands of Schillinger Company Household Terms in Birmingham." April 23, 1900.

————. "Brewers Hop on Red Beer Boom to Spur Flat Sales." August 10, 1995.

————. "Business Notes." April 13, 1995.

BIBLIOGRAPHY

———. "Cahaba Brewing Sets Opening." September 29, 2012.

———. "City's Brewing Industry Goes Back to 1884." July 13, 2000.

———. "Fine Beer: The New Brewery Is a Modern One." June 5, 1897.

———. "First Lager Beer Brewery in Alabama and Its History." July 1, 1903.

———. "Freshfully Wins Contest, Free Rent for Food Store." March 31, 2012.

———. "Local Ale Wins Medal." April 3, 1998.

———. "Looking Back: City's First Mardi Gras." February 1, 1959.

———. "New Brew from Vulcan Wins Medal." October 17, 1997.

———. "6-Months Rent Offered to Biz." January 7, 2012.

Birmingham News-Age Herald. "Avondale History Colorful." January 27, 1929.

Birmingham Post-Herald. "Pot Luck: Breckenridge Brewery Is the New Bright Spot in Southside." January 15, 1997.

Blalock, Bob. "Why Does Freeing Hops, Other Bills, Take So Long?" *Birmingham News,* June 7, 2009.

Brown, Melissa. "A Backwards Step: Small Towns Left in Limbo by Alcohol Sales Ruling." AL.com, March 4, 2015.

Brownfield, Andy, Associated Press. "Beer Fans Await Action on Bill for Home Brewing." *Birmingham News,* May 15, 2012.

———. "Brew in Bigger Bottles? It's in Bentley's Hands." *Huntsville Times,* May 15, 2012.

Cahill, Kendra. "Beer Connoisseurs Deserve Same Rights as Wine Lovers." *Birmingham News,* letter to the editor, February 14, 2006.

Carlton, Bob. "Drawing a Cold One: City Welcomes First Brew Pub." *Birmingham News,* March 9, 1995.

———. "5 Birmingham Bars Make *Southern Living* Best List." *Birmingham News,* January 24, 2014.

———. "Japan Meets Mexico: 'Simple, Fun and Creative.'" *Birmingham News,* October 15, 2014.

———. "Owners of Saw's Soul Kitchen to Open Pizza Shop." *Birmingham News,* November 10, 2013.

———. "Saw's Adds a Little Soul (Food) in Avondale." *Birmingham News,* March 30, 2012.

———. "Soppin' Allowed: City Boasts Own Taste in Vittles." *Birmingham News,* March 24, 1995.

Cason, Mike. "A Brewing Debate." *Birmingham News,* February 22, 2013.

Cason, Mike, and Kim Chandler. "House Crafts a Yes Vote for Personal Use." *Birmingham News,* April 3, 2013.

Chandler, Kim. "Cheers! Home Brewing Legal in Alabama, Governor Signs Bill; State Was Nation's Final Holdout." *Birmingham News,* May 10, 2013.

———. "Debate Brews Over Pitch for Fancy Beer." *Birmingham News,* February 12, 2006.

————. "Higher-Alcohol Beer Bill Hops Over a High Hurdle." *Birmingham News*, May 15, 2009.

————. "Home Brew May Become Legal." *Birmingham News*, April 27, 2012.

————. "House OKs Bill to Allow Sale of More Potent Beers." *Birmingham News*, March 5, 2008.

————. "Panel Gives Beer Bill Stout Support." *Birmingham News*, March 22, 2007.

Childers, James Saxon. "Miss Fancy Decides to Tell All." *Birmingham News-Age Herald*, March 25, 1934.

Cold Storage and Ice Trade Journal, November 1905.

Colurso, Mary. "Cracking Open Cask & Drum: Newcomer to Festival Lineup Promises Music, Wine, Beer for Lakeview District." *Birmingham News*, August 14, 2013.

————. "DJs Meet Southern Rock." *Birmingham News*, July 9, 2014.

Conway, Chris. "She Was City's Pride." *Birmingham Post-Herald*, July 15, 1968.

Crabtree, Shona. "A Matter of Taste: Beer and Wine Connoisseurs Seek Out Home-Brewed Flavor." *Mobile Register*, July 14, 1995.

Crowley, John. J., Jr. "Have a Nice National Homebrew Day." *Huntsville Times*, letter to the editor, April 13, 1997.

Cure, Sarah. "4 Micro-Breweries, 4th Largest City in State: Huntsville Leads the Craft Beer Explosion." *Huntsville Times*, October 17, 2010.

————. "Nook and Stem & Stein Get National Honors." *Huntsville Times*, January 26, 2012.

Davis, Bryan. "Beer Engineers Construction to Begin This Summer." *Birmingham Business Journal*, May 28, 2014.

————. "Beer Engineers Plans February Completion at Railroad Park." *Birmingham Business Journal*, October 23, 2014.

————. "HudsonAlpha Firm Strikes Deal with Back Forty Beer." *Birmingham Business Journal*, July 2, 2014.

————. "7 Questions with AlaBev President Harry Kampakis." *Birmingham Business Journal*, March 18, 2014.

————. "Seven Thoughts with AlaBev's Matt Kilpatrick." *Birmingham Business Journal*, October 20, 2014.

Debro, Anita. "Gourmet Beer Could Take a Week to Hit Store Shelves." *Birmingham News*, May 23, 2009.

————. "Heady Days Arrive for Specialty Beers: New State Law Allows Higher-Alcohol Brews." *Birmingham News*, May 23, 2009.

Diel, Stan. "Alabama Craft Brewing Industry Has Room to Grow." *Birmingham News*, August 30, 2013.

————. "All This Just for a Beer: After Miles of Red Tape, Brewpub Opening Planned Here in Late February." *Birmingham News*, October 27, 1994.

————. "Another Brewery Is on Tap for the Railroad Park Area." *Birmingham News*, April 17, 2013.

————. "Avondale Brewing Begins Bottling." *Birmingham News*, September 15, 2013.

————. "Avondale Brewing Co.'s First Bottled Beer Released." *Birmingham News*, October 6, 2013.

————. "Avondale Brewing's Bottling Plans Delayed." *Birmingham News*, May 17, 2013.

————. "Avondale Hopes for New Tenants." *Birmingham News*, January 19, 2012.

————. "Bama's Brewing Boom: State's Beer Production Has Doubled Every Year Since 2009." *Huntsville Times*, February 22, 2013.

————. "Beer Distributor Endorses Home-Brew Bill." *Birmingham News*, February 13, 2013.

————. "Beer Lovers' Store Brewing." *Birmingham News*, December 15, 2011.

————. "Beer Wave Alert: City Impact This Summer." *Birmingham News*, June 7, 2012.

————. "Beer Will Finally Flow in Avondale." *Birmingham News*, November 3, 2011.

————. "Brewers with State Ties to Sell Beer Here." *Birmingham News*, June 21, 2012.

————. "Brewery Site Shifts from Downtown to Lakeview." *Birmingham News*, March 15, 2013.

————. "Brewpub's Sales Plunge Amid Confused Rumors of Closing." *Birmingham News*, October 24, 1996.

————. "Cigar City Brewing Adds Ale Inspired by State Beer Laws." *Birmingham News*, October 25, 2013.

————. "Committee OKs Outdoor Concert Stage at Avondale Brewing Co." *Birmingham News*, April 12, 2013.

————. "Distributor Carrying More Oskar Blues Beers in City." *Birmingham News*, August 29, 2012.

————. "Good People Beer Flies Off Shelves Quickly." *Birmingham News*, March 10, 2011.

————. "Good People Expands Brewery." *Birmingham News*, January 23, 2013.

————. "Highland Drafts Runneth Over: Package Store Expands." *Birmingham News*, November 13, 2010.

————. "Hop City to Add Covered Patio." *Birmingham News*, April 28, 2013.

————. "Late-Night Hopping for Bigger Beer: New Law Allows 25.4 Ounces." *Birmingham News*, August 2, 2012.

————. "Making the Big Bucks from Beer: Alabama Beer Distributors Report Tallies Distributors' Economic Impact." *Birmingham News*, March 17, 2013.

BIBLIOGRAPHY

————. "New Beer in a Month—No Foolin'." *Birmingham News*, March 3, 2011.

————. "New Craft Beers Hitting Shelves Wednesday: New Law Allows Bigger 25.4 Ounce Bottle." *Birmingham News*, July 27, 2012.

————. "Restaurant, Brewery Set for Barber Spot." *Birmingham News*, May 10, 2012.

————. "Slice to Make More Room for Its Brews." *Birmingham News*, June 28, 2012.

————. "So You Think You Can Brew? To Celebrate New Law, Local Budweiser Set to Sponsor Home-Brewing Contest." *Birmingham News*, May 26, 2013.

————. "Tanks Arrive for Southside Brewery, Tap Room: Will Likely Produce 1,500 to 2,000 Barrels a Year." *Birmingham News*, September 6, 2013.

————. "'Thirsty' Birmingham to See Craft Brewery Raise Its First Glass by October." *Birmingham News*, August 18, 2013.

————. "Vestavia Hills Man's Cream Ale Wins Brew Contest." *Birmingham News*, October 6, 2013.

————. "Vulcan Breweries Stock Will Be on Tap at Web Site." *Birmingham News*, July 23, 1997.

Dobbs, Jay. "Homebrewing Bill Will Boost Business." *Birmingham Business Journal*, February 22, 2013.

Doyle, Steve. "Thirst for Craft Beer Has Never Been Stronger, but Are Alabama Breweries Turning a Profit?" AL.com, February 4, 2015.

Dugan, Kelli. "Brewing in Alabama, by the Numbers." (Mobile, AL) *Press-Register*, July 27, 2014.

————. "What's Brewing in Alabama?" (Mobile, AL) *Press-Register*, July 30, 2014.

Edgar, David. "Craft Brewing: Fastest Growth in the Industry." *New Brewer*, 1995.

Ehinger, John. "Better Beers." *Huntsville Times*, March 24, 2007.

Eipers, Peter. "Free the Hops Bill Passes a Hurdle." *Birmingham News*, letter to the editor, March 10, 2008.

————. "Ignorance Led to Bill's Defeat." *Birmingham News*, letter to the editor, April 10, 2007.

Estes, Cary. "Hearty and American as Free Enterprise." *Business Alabama*, February 2014.

Faulk, Kent. "Comedy Central Savors Cullman's Dry Oktoberfest." *Birmingham News*, October 4, 2005.

Fromson, Daniel. "Die of the Week: Mapping the Rise of Craft Beer." Newyorker.com, June 6, 2013.

Gaskin, Tom. "Magic City Brewery Beer 'Head' and Shoulders Above Any Other." *Birmingham News*, October 17, 1997.

Geiss, Chuck. "Naked Birmingham." *Black & White City Paper*, April 28, 2011.

Godwin, Brent. "Alabama One Step Closer to Legal Homebrewing." *Birmingham Business Journal*, May 8, 2013.

———. "Avondale Rolls Out Second Bottled Brew." *Birmingham Business Journal*, November 5, 2013.

———. "Best Craft Beer in Alabama? *Southern Living* Says Good People IPA." *Birmingham Business Journal*, May 19, 2014.

———. "Burr & Forman's Sellers Earns Beer Certification." *Birmingham Business Journal*, December 13, 2013.

———. "Craft Beer Had $238M Economic Impact on Alabama." *Birmingham Business Journal*, January 6, 2014.

———. "CraftBeer Recognizes UAB as 'Obsessed.'" *Birmingham Business Journal*, September 11, 2013.

———. "5 Thoughts with Back Forty Beer President Jason Wilson." *Birmingham Business Journal*. May 13, 2014.

———. "Which Beer Best Represents Alabama?" *Birmingham Business Journal*, August 9, 2013.

Graham, Gloria P. "Old Vulcan Gets His Own Beer Brand." *Birmingham Post-Herald*, August 15, 1997.

Gray, David. "BBJ Wasted Valuable Space on Beer Editorial." *Birmingham Business Journal*, letter to the editor, February 15, 2009.

Guttery, Mason. "Tell Lawmakers: We Want Better Beer." *Birmingham News*, letter to the editor, March 3, 2009.

Harmon, Rick. "Acclaimed Pale Ale Returns to Alabama: Oskar Blues Started in an Auburn Bathtub." *Montgomery Advertiser*, July 5, 2012.

Harvey, Alec. "Avondale Brewers' Labors Come to a Head: Brewfest Will Be the Debut for New Beers." *Birmingham News*, June 3, 2011.

———. "Have a Beer—or Have Your Pick." *Birmingham News*, June 1, 2012.

———. "Think You Know Alabama Beer? Try Our Quiz First, Smartypants." *Birmingham News*, August 8, 2014.

Harvey, Fletcher. "Breckenridge Dining So Fresh a Freezer Isn't Necessary." *Birmingham News*, December 20, 1996.

———. "Cellar Entrees Run Hot and Cold, Literally and Figuratively." *Birmingham News*, January 24, 1997.

———. "Much More on Tap than Beer at the Magic City Brewery." *Birmingham News*, April 20, 1995.

Henckell, R.B. "80 Magic Years of Progress." *Birmingham History Semi-Centennial*, December 1951.

Hollis, Guy. "Do Smiling Mug Shots and Liquor Mix?" *Huntsville Times*, September 4, 1994.

Hollis, Mike. "Repeal Home-Brewing Ban." *Huntsville Times*, editorial, September 25, 2012.

Horn, Jason. "The New Neighborhood Brew." *Birmingham* magazine, March 2011.

Hough, Jere. "'Brew Buddies' Enjoy Making Their Own Ale." (Mobile, AL) *Press-Register,* June 7, 2009.

Howell, Vickii. "Grant to Spur Fight Against Blight: Group Gets $40 Million to Help Neighborhoods." *Birmingham News*, April 20, 2003.

Huggins, Paul. "Political Leverage Helped Rescue Home-Brew Bill: Holtzclaw Offers Behind-Scenes Look at How Bill Passed." *Huntsville Times*, September 15, 2013.

Huntsville Times. "Beer Buffs to Roll Out the Bottle." July 28, 2012.

Jamison, John. "Miss Fancy Hospitable on Anniversary." *Birmingham News*, October 13, 1933.

Jimmerson, Janet. "Network Spotlights Area Eateries." *Birmingham Post-Herald*, February 24, 2000.

Jimmerson, Janet, and Christine Jacobs. "Magic City Brewery Expands Menu." *Birmingham Post-Herald*, June 9, 1999.

Johnson, Bob, Associated Press. "Bill Passes to Allow Higher-Alcohol Beers." *Birmingham News*, March 5, 2008.

———. "House OKs Bill Allowing More Potent Beers." *Birmingham News*, March 4, 2009.

Jordan, Phillip. "Have You Seen These Beers?" *Birmingham Weekly*, April 7, 2005.

Kaylor, Mike. "Breckenridge Brewery." *Huntsville Times*, November 6, 1997.

Kearley, Theodore F. "Thanks, Senator." *Huntsville Times*, letter to the editor, May 1, 2007.

Kent, Dawn. "Gourmet Suds Giving a Jolt to Birmingham-Area Businesses." *Birmingham News*, June 5, 2009.

Kindred, Ingrid. "Birmingham's First Brewery Since '07 Now Offering Tours." *Birmingham News*, November 3, 1992.

Kizzire, Jamie. "$4 Million Renovation Planned: Young & Vann to Become Wee Care." *Birmingham Post-Herald*, July 10, 2001.

Lindley, Tom. "Homemade Beer Taboo in State and Kits Are Too, ABC Execs Say." *Birmingham News*, March 6, 1994.

Lowry, Bob. "Beer Bill Backers Can Taste Victory." *Huntsville Times*, March 11, 2007.

———. "House Panel Says Yes to Higher-Alcohol Beer." *Huntsville Times*, March 22, 2007.

Matthews, Michelle. "Colorful Businesses, Colorful CEOs." *Business Alabama*, October 2012.

Maynard, Melissa, McClatchy Tribune. "Beers and Cheers." *Birmingham News*, May 26, 2013.

McAlister, Laura, Joe O'Donnell, Mary Ellen Stancill and Carla Jean Whitley. "The Drinker's Dozen." *Birmingham* magazine, August 2009.

BIBLIOGRAPHY

McClendon, Robert. "Craft Brewers Look to Sell Beer Right to Consumers." *Huntsville Times*. April 14, 2013.

———. "Mobile County Prosecutor Disciplined for Home Brewing." *Huntsville Times*, March 20, 2013.

McLaughlin, Budd. "Oskar Blues Coming to Alabama." *Huntsville Times*, June 28, 2012.

(Mobile, AL) *Press-Register*. "Update Liquor Laws to Allow Bigger Bottles." March 2, 2012.

Mobile Register. "Low Alcoholic Content Found for Home Brew." December 12, 1999.

———. "Microbrewery Looks for Buyer." August 13, 1996.

———. "Turner Supply to Get Young & Vann Assets." June 25, 2000.

Murphy, Dan. "Avondale Brewing Co. Bringing Life to a Historic Birmingham Neighborhood." *Birmingham News*, April 5, 2012.

———. "Brewery Modernization Act Passes the House." (Mobile, AL) *Press-Register*, June 2, 2011.

———. "Free the Hops Looks to Remove Bottle Size Restriction When Lawmakers Convene Feb. 7." (Mobile, AL) *Press-Register*, February 2, 2012.

———. "Good Things Are Brewing in Birmingham." (Mobile, AL) *Press-Register*, March 22, 2012.

———. "Looking to the Future for Alabama's Breweries, Brewpubs." (Mobile, AL) *Press-Register*, June 9, 2011.

———. "'Maybe Next Year' for State's Brewers and Brew Pubs." (Mobile, AL) *Press-Register*, April 29, 2010.

———. "Truck Stop Honey Earns Silver at GABF." (Mobile, AL) *Press-Register*, September 30, 2010.

———. "We Beat Mississippi: It's No Longer a Felony to Home-Brew." (Mobile, AL) *Press-Register*, May 10, 2013.

———. "What's Brewing." (Mobile, AL) *Press-Register*, May 5, 2011.

Murtaugh, Dan. "Barrels of Trouble: Beer Battle Foams Over." (Mobile, AL) *Press-Register*, April 23, 2011.

———. "Homebrewers Hope Success of Free the Hops Bodes Well for Them." (Mobile, AL) *Press-Register*, June 9, 2009.

Nabbefeld, Joe. "Beer Maker Expands Brew List to 7 with Bock." *Birmingham News*, February 14, 1996.

———. "Birmingham Building Prepared for Brewpub." *Birmingham News*, August 24, 1994.

Newberry, Trevor. "Crafting a Family of Beers." *Birmingham*, June 2013.

———. "Upping the Ante." *Birmingham* magazine, May 2011.

Normingtom, Mick. "Preparing to Jump into Suds Business." *Birmingham News*, December 29, 1994.

Peck, John. "Where Will Olde Towne Rise Again?" *Huntsville Times*, July 7, 2007.

Phillips, Ryan. "Cahaba Brewing Co. Growth Signals Downtown Revitalization." *Birmingham Business Journal*, October 15, 2014.

———. "Craft Beer Production Surges in State." *Birmingham Business Journal*, August 4, 2014.

———. "Gadsden's Back Forty Ranked One of Best Local Breweries in U.S." *Birmingham Business Journal*, August 7, 2014.

———. "Good People Brewing Co. Establishes Laboratory at Innovation Depot." *Birmingham Business Journal*, September 4, 2014.

———. "Top States for Beer: Where Does Alabama Rank?" *Birmingham Business Journal*, August 27, 2014.

Plott, Bill. "Barbecue Backs Free the Hops." *Birmingham News*, September 8, 2006.

———. "Beer Bill Dies, but Advocates Make Headway." *Birmingham News*, July 5, 2006.

———. "Cheers to the Judge! UAB Researcher Spends Spare Time Ranking Beer." *Birmingham News*. November 7, 2000.

———. "City's Brewing Industry Goes Back to 1884." *Birmingham News*, July 13, 2000.

———. "City's Last Brewery to Shut Down as New Owners Move Operations." *Birmingham News*, July 13, 2000.

———. "Disc Golf Tournament on Par with Free the Hops Barbecue." *Birmingham News*, September 10, 2006.

———. "Free the Hops President Resigns; Successor Named." *Birmingham News*, January 4, 2008.

———. "Gourmet Beer Fans Want World-Class Brews in State." *Birmingham News*, June 23, 2005.

———. "Little Star Gets Bigger with New Brew." *Birmingham News*, July 9, 1999.

———. "Magic City Brewery Tapped Out." *Birmingham News*, June 20, 2000.

———. "Mobile Brewery Tests Pub Market: Mr. Jim's Tries to Whet Taste for Flat Industry." *Birmingham News*, March 5, 2004.

———. "Olde Towne's Brewing Ale and Hearty Business." *Birmingham News*, April 1, 2005.

———. "State Lawmaker Says Bringing in Higher-Alcohol Beers Will Take Time." *Birmingham News*, August 24, 2005.

———. "Where's the Beer? There Will Be Plenty on Tap at Brewfest at Sloss Furnaces This Weekend." *Birmingham News*, June 1, 2007.

———. "Vulcan Beer Returning to Store Shelves." *Birmingham News*, July 9, 1999.

Poe, Kelly. "Closed for Renovations." *Birmingham News*, February 15, 2015.

———. "Company Launching Canned Beer Line." *Birmingham News*, November 7, 2014.

Poe, Ryan. "Alabama Is Feeling the Effects of Beer Business." *Birmingham Business Journal*, February 25, 2013.

BIBLIOGRAPHY

————. "Birmingham Brewers Craft Expansion Plans." *Birmingham Business Journal*, October 26, 2012.

————. "Breweries Tapping into Birmingham." *Birmingham Business Journal*, April 20, 2012.

————. "New Downtown Brewery on Tap for Beer Engineers." *Birmingham Business Journal*, December 21, 2012.

Post-Herald Bureau. "Gov. Wallace Finally Gets Wine Bill." *Birmingham Post-Herald*, August 31, 1973.

Powell, J.E., Jr. "Larger Means Get Drunk Quicker." *Birmingham News*, letter to the editor, February 29, 2012.

Prather, David, and John Ehinger. "Just Stay Off the Phone." *Huntsville Times*, March 24, 2007.

Pratt, Ted. "Internet Beer Stock Interest Cheers Officials." *Birmingham News*, August 19, 1997.

Rawls, Phillip, Associated Press. "Alcohol Bills Flowing." *Birmingham News*, May 15, 2009.

————. "Beer Buffs Toast Passage of Brew Pub Bill." *Birmingham News*, June 2, 2011.

————. "Bill Would OK Stronger Beers." *Birmingham News*, February 12, 2009.

————. "Senate May Discuss Bill to Legalize Stronger Beer." *Birmingham News*, May 17, 2008.

Reyonlds, Ed. "Where the Beers Are." *Black & White City Paper*, May 31, 2007.

Rupinski, Patrick. "New Beers Birmingham-Bound." *Birmingham Post-Herald*, February 10, 1996.

Schauer, Roman. "Sloss Will Overflow with Suds for Brewfest." *Birmingham Post-Herald*, October 20, 1995.

Shipley, Jonathan. "The United States of Beer: Alabama." *Poor Taste Magazine*, March 6, 2011.

Simon, Stephanie. "Bible Belt Battle Brewing Over Beer." *LA Times*, March 30, 2008.

Sirmon, Greg. "Gourmet Beer Will Increase Choices." *Mobile Register*, letter to the editor, February 18, 2009.

Spencer, Thomas. "City Brewers Oppose Mine on Mulberry Fork." *Birmingham News*, January 27, 2012.

————. "Free the Hops Wants Bud Boycott." *Birmingham News*, February 1, 2008.

————. "Magic City Tale, Good and Bad, Soon to Be Told: Museum Will Place Focus on Area's History." *Birmingham News*, December 27, 2009.

————. "There's Beer Brewing Again in Birmingham: Good People Beer Co. Rolls Barrel Out Slowly." *Birmingham News*, July 19, 2008.

Stein, Kelsey. "One 'Hip' Little Neighborhood: *Southern Living* Magazine Recognition Drawing Out-of-Town Visitors." *Birmingham News*, April 10, 2013.

———. "Website: Good People Makes State's Best-Known Brew." *Birmingham News*, July 14, 2013.

Stephens, Challen. "Great Beer Debate." *Huntsville Times*, January 15, 2006.

St. Onge, Peter. "Brewpub Coming to Downtown Area." *Huntsville Times*, March 17, 1996.

———. "Persistence Keeps Plans Brewing." *Huntsville Times*, March 7, 1997.

Stromberg, Joseph. "America's Taste in Beer, in Five Maps." Vox.com, May 17, 2014 (accessed January 3, 2015).

Stroud, Matt. "Is Free Rent Enough to Jumpstart a Sleepy Commercial District?" Citylab.com, October 22, 2012 (accessed January 3, 2015).

Sutton, Amber. "Taste Alabama One Hop at a Time." (Mobile, AL) *Press-Register*, April 14, 2013.

Swant, Martin. "Bill Would Make Homebrewing Legal." *Huntsville Times*, January 23, 2013.

———. "Occupy Avondale Winner to Be Announced." *Birmingham News*, March 24, 2012.

———. "State Beer Tax Is 2nd Highest." *Birmingham News*, March 10, 2012.

———. "Will Crenshaw, Future Master Brewer for Trim Tab Brewhouse." *Birmingham News*, July 1, 2012.

———. "World of Beer Plans Birmingham Locations." *Birmingham News*, May 9, 2012.

Taylor, Beverly. "Microbrewery Growth Sparks Interest in Complexity of Beers." *Birmingham News*, November 6, 1996.

Taylor, Rebecca. "Eating Out: Magic City Brewery Opening March 10." *Birmingham Post-Herald*, March 1, 1995.

Temple, Chanda. "Citizens Group Backs Tax Proposal: Plan Hits Concerns, Region 2020 Says." *Birmingham News*, June 20, 2003.

Thorne, Christopher. "It's a Heady Business, but It Can Go Flat Fast." *Birmingham Post-Herald*, February 12, 1998.

Thornton, Trey. "Bigger Beer Bottles Not Such a Good Idea." (Mobile, AL) *Press-Register*, letter to the editor, March 21, 2012.

Tomberlin, Michael. "Alabama Media Group Moving Birmingham Offices." *Birmingham News*, September 27, 2013.

———. "Alabama's Beer Industry Buzzing." *Birmingham News*, July 5, 2013.

———. "Beer Container Bill Comes to a Head, Faces Vote in House." *Birmingham News*, April 13, 2012.

———. "Beer Distributor Birmingham Beverage, after 107 Years, Rebrands Itself as AlaBev." *Birmingham News*, May 14, 2014.

———. "Bentley OK's Bigger Beer Bottles." *Birmingham News*, May 17, 2012.

———. "Bigger Beer Container Bill Awaits House Vote." *Birmingham News*, April 14, 2012.

————. "Birmingham Budweiser Seeks Bigger Site." *Birmingham News*, April 8, 2005.

————. "Birmingham's Trim Tab Launches Its First Summer Seasonal Beer." *Birmingham News*, June 1, 2014.

————. "Brewers Hopping to the Alabama Suds Rush." *Birmingham News*, October 14, 2010.

————. "Brewer's Investigation Tracks Stolen Kegs: Intruders Stole Dozens of Metal Kegs for Scrap." *Birmingham News*, June 12, 2011.

————. "Brewery on Rise as Popularity Overflows." *Birmingham News*, May 20, 2010.

————. "Brewing Up Bigger Beers in Alabama: Legislature Weighs Larger Containers." *Birmingham News*, February 25, 2012.

————. "Center of Change: Old Young & Vann Building Becomes New Center for Regional Planning and Design." *Birmingham News*, August 24, 2003.

————. "Freeing More Hops." *Birmingham News*, February 23, 2012.

————. "Free the Hops Calls Boycott." *Birmingham News*, April 23, 2011.

————. "Free the Hops Pushing for Bigger Beers." *Birmingham News*, February 25, 2012.

————. "Good News for Birmingham Brews." *Birmingham News*, January 19, 2014.

————. "Good People Brewing Canning Popular Coffee Oatmeal Stout." *Birmingham News*, January 19, 2014.

————. "Google 'Birmingham Beer' E-Commerce: Good People Brewing Tapped to Tell Its Story after Doubling Business in a Year." *Birmingham News*, July 25, 2014.

————. "Gov. Bentley Plans to Sign Beer Bill into Law." *Birmingham News*, June 9, 2011.

————. "Grassroots Beer Lovers, Wholesalers Compromise." *Birmingham News*, May 3, 2011.

————. "Group Aims to Free the Brewers State Bill Seeks Deregulation." *Birmingham News*, January 24, 2010.

————. "Meanwhile the State's Largest Homegrown Brewery Is Getting Bigger." *Birmingham News*, March 9, 2014.

————. "New Hub of Activity." *Birmingham News*, March 23, 2014.

————. "New in the Brew Beer Industry: Birmingham's Trim Tab Has the Area's First Female Brewer." *Birmingham News*, March 2, 2014.

————. "Parkside District Plans Warming Up: City Looks to Future Ballpark to Drive Mixed-Use Project." *Birmingham News*, January 4, 2012.

————. "Taller Boys Heading This Way: New Alabama Law Allows 25.4 Ounce Bottles of Beer." *Birmingham News*, May 17, 2012.

————. "Thirst Quencher Parkside District: Beer Engineers Start Work on $5M Brewery, Taproom, Restaurant." *Birmingham News*, May 30, 2014.

———. "Trail of Suds Brewing Industry: Inaugural Tour Spotlights Birmingham-Made Craft Beer." *Birmingham News*, April 30, 2014.

———. "Winery Group Presses Boycott of Beer Distributors." *Birmingham News*, April 20, 2012.

Tomberlin, Michael, and Dawn Kent. "State Breweries Close to Tapping into Brewpubs: Law Would Allow What Breweries in Other States Do." *Birmingham News*, May 12, 2011.

Tortorano, David. "Small Breweries Taste Success Again: Some 120 Microbreweries Produce about 15,000 Barrels a Year." *Mobile Register*, May 16, 1993.

Tuggle, Kathryn. "Cheers to Beers: Alabama Raises a Glass to Home-Brew, Brewfest and Craft Breweries." *Birmingham News*, June 2, 2013.

Underwood, Madison. "Bring on the Brew: Cahaba Brewery, Hop City Unite in Effort to Legalize Homebrewing." *Birmingham News*, February 27, 2013.

———. "Home-Brewing Seizure Not 'Raid,' ABC Says." *Birmingham News*, September 22, 2012.

Vance, Billy. "Size Allows for Gourmet Beers." *Birmingham News*, letter to the editor, March 2, 2012.

Velasco, Eric. "Bask in the Cask: Brewfest to Add Cask Ales This Year." *Birmingham News*, June 4, 2010.

———. "Building a Beer Scene: The J. Clyde Tavern and Alehouse Has Been a Central Figure in the City's Craft Beer Movement." *Birmingham* magazine, April 2014.

———. "Drive and Drink: To Get a Bottle of Good People's New Label, County Line, Go East." *Birmingham News*, November 21, 2010.

———. "New Alcohol Law Sparks Draft Beer-to-Go Buzz in Area." *Birmingham News*, February 22, 2010.

Vickery, Scottie. "If the Brew Fits…Like Beer? You Can Go to the Head of This Class." *Birmingham News*, August 29, 1994.

Wake, Matt. "Final Beer in Liberation Series Celebrates Gourmet Bottle Bill." *Huntsville Times*, February 8, 2013.

Wallen, Paul. "Gourmet Bottle Bill Goes to Governor." *Huntsville Times*, May 10, 2012.

Walsh, Alex. "Avondale Grows: More Parking, Another Restaurant." *Birmingham News*, March 22, 2013.

———. "Business Is Brewing." *Birmingham News*, May 15, 2013.

———. "Good People Brewery Expects Ballpark to Be a Good Neighbor: Traffic into the Business Will Most Likely Increase." *Birmingham News*, March 1, 2013.

———. "Home Buying Is Up Sharply in East Birmingham Neighborhoods." *Birmingham News*, April 10, 2013.

———. "How Many Craft Breweries Can Alabama Sustain?" *Birmingham News*, August 25, 2013.

Walsh, Maggie Hall. "High Overhead Closes Southside Brew Pub." *Birmingham News*, August 25, 1998.

Warren, Carol Robinson. "Profits Sizzle as Heat Climbs." *Birmingham News*, July 23, 1993.

West, Ty. "BBJ Flashback: 5 Projects that Could Transform Downtown Birmingham." *Birmingham Business Journal*, June 4, 2013.

———. "Beer Engineers to Brew Up More Jobs in 2014." *Birmingham Business Journal*, December 19, 2013.

Whitley, Carla Jean. "Ale for Sale." *Birmingham* magazine, September 2007.

———. "Best Bars in Birmingham." *Birmingham* magazine, March 2012.

———. "Exceeding Expectations." *Birmingham* magazine, October 2010.

———. "Hops for Honeys: Women's Beer Groups Take Off." *Paste*, September 10, 2014. http://www.pastemagazine.com/blogs/lists/2014/09/hops-for-honeys-womens-beer-groups-take-off.html (accessed December 30, 2014).

———. "Know Your Beer: Birmingham-Area Beer Professionals Have Obtained an Academic Standing of Craft Beer." *Birmingham* magazine, March 2014.

———. "The Perfect Blend." *Alabama Alumni Magazine* (Winter 2014).

———. "Smart Living Guide to Bar Hopping." *Birmingham* magazine, July 2007.

———. "Sweet Home Alabama." *Sky* magazine, June 2013.

———. "A Tale of Two Neighborhoods." *Birmingham* magazine, September 2012.

Whittington, George. "Wreckers Sound Taps for Old Brewery Here, Long Since Dry; It's 'High Life' Was Short One." *Birmingham News*, February 17, 1952.

Wilkinson, Kaija. "Move Over, Miller." (Mobile, AL) *Press-Register*, October 11, 2009.

———. "Third Time's a Charm?" (Mobile, AL) *Press-Register*, January 21, 2007.

Williams, Roy L. "'The Beers Are Made for Those that Enjoy Quality over Quantity, Full, Robust Flavors over Thin, Bland Beers…'" *Birmingham News*, September 16, 2010.

———. "Birmingham Brewing Sold to Investor Group." *Birmingham News*, December 13, 1996.

———. "City's Second Brewery to Bring Hops to Avondale." *Birmingham News*, June 24, 2010.

———. "Help Wanted: Wine Expert." *Birmingham News*, September 20, 1999.

———. "New Businesses." *Birmingham News*, November 19, 1996.

———. "Time Constraints Force Brewery Owner to Sell." *Birmingham News*, August 13, 1996.

Wilson, Wesley W. "Connoisseurs, Not Drunks." *Huntsville Times*, letter to the editor, April 8, 2007.

Bibliography

Websites and Blogs

Alabama Legislative Information System Online. http://alisondb.legislature. state.al.us (accessed February 14, 2015).

Alabama Properties Listed on the National Register of Historic Places as of February 20, 2014. www.preserveala.org/pdfs/TAX_CREDIT/New_ Folder/List_NR_Properties_n_AL.pdf (accessed February 14, 2015).

Brewers Association. http://brewersassociation.org (accessed January 31, 2015).

Free the Hops restrictions. http://www.freethehops.org/restrictions (accessed January 1, 2015).

"How a Bill Becomes a Law." Alabama Secretary of State Kids Pages. http://www.sos.alabama.gov/kids/bill.htm (accessed March 10, 2015).

Old Breweries. oldbreweries.com (accessed February 14, 2015).

Roberts, Dan. "About the Boycott." http://www.freethehops.org/ blog/2011/04/about-the-boycott (accessed February 22, 2015).

———. "Details of the Substitute." http://www.freethehops.org/ blog/2011/05/details-of-the-substitute (accessed February 22, 2015).

"A Short History of AlaBev." http://alabev.com/about/history (accessed December 30, 2014).

"Timeline of Brewing in Alabama." http://alabev.com/alabama-beer-scene/timeline (accessed December 30, 2014).

Wilson, Brad. "10 Defining Moments in Modern Alabama Craft Beer." http://backfortybeer.com/barn/post/10_defining_moments_in_ modern_alabama_craft_beer (accessed February 14, 2015).

Other Sources

Beer Engineers Twitter account. twitter.com/beerengineers (accessed March 1, 2015).

Directory of Manufacturers and Buyers Guide of Birmingham District Alabama. Birmingham, AL: Manufacturers Association of Birmingham, 1908. Southern History Collection, Birmingham Public Library, Department of Archives and Manuscripts.

1887 Pocket Business Directory and Guide to Birmingham, Ala. Monograph, 1887. Birmingham, Alabama Directories. Birmingham Suburban Area Directories. Birmingham Public Library, Department of Archives and Manuscripts.

"In the South." *American Bottler* (January 1907).

Lake, Hunter. Avondale Brewing Company history. N.d.

Plott, Bill. Alabama Breweries chronology. N.d.

"Spirited Away." *The Daily Show.* Comedy Central. New York, October 18, 2005.

Wahl, Arnold Spencer, and Robert Wahl. "Corporation Affairs." In *American Brewers' Review.* Chicago: Der Braumeister Pub. Co., 1887–1939.

INDEX

Index

ABOUT THE AUTHOR

Carla Jean Whitley is a writer, editor and teacher based in Birmingham, Alabama, where she is a features reporter for Alabama Media Group. Carla Jean, a craft beer enthusiast, joined women's craft beer education group Hops for Honeys in 2010. She volunteers with literacy organizations and teaches journalism at the University of Alabama and Samford University. Her favorite yoga pose is bakasana, and her favorite cats are orange. She is also the author of *Muscle Shoals Sound Studio: How the Swampers Changed American Music* and *Balancing Act: Yoga Essays*. Connect with her at carlajeanwhitley.com.

Photo by Cheryl Joy Miner.

Visit us at
www.historypress.net
....
This title is also available as an e-book